CHRISTIANITY AND INTERNATIONAL PEACE

SIX LECTURES AT GRINNELL COLLEGE,
GRINNELL, IOWA, IN FEBRUARY, 1915,
ON THE GEORGE A. GATES MEMORIAL
FOUNDATION

BY

CHARLES EDWARD JEFFERSON

PASTOR OF THE BROADWAY TABERNACLE
IN NEW YORK CITY

NEW YORK
THOMAS Y. CROWELL COMPANY
PUBLISHERS

CONTENTS

CHRISTIANITY AND INTERNATIONAL PEACE

I

The Greatest Problem of the Twentieth Century

WE are living in the age of the social question. Humanity has at last worked its way into the public eye. The relations of man to man, of groups of men to groups of men, of corporations or bodies of men to other corporations, these are to-day the subject of the world's chief concern. How to live together is the sovereign problem upon which the most thoughtful minds are focused. How to get rid of the social evils by which humanity is scourged and hampered, is a problem from which the most sensitive hearts are unable to get away.

9

And so we are living in an age of social remedies, solutions, panaceas. Innumerable reformers have gone abroad, each one enthusiastic over some particular method to bring about the social reconstruction for which the world is to-day in travail. Numberless books exploit schemes of social welfare. Many prophets are preaching almost furiously a gospel of social redemption. Men search the New Testament for a social gospel, and Jesus is discovered to be a social reformer. His idea of the kingdom has been found to be the central idea of all his teaching, and this idea is working like a mighty ferment in the heart of our generation. The whole Church of Christ is being carried onward as on a tidal wave toward issues larger than any it has ever faced since the Reformation. With the social idea before them, men are taking a quickened interest in all the kingdoms of life; the family, society, business, recreation, education, art, literature, politics. We are coming to see that these are the kingdoms which are to become the kingdoms of Christ. They can become his kingdoms only through our coöperation. They are areas of life which we by his help must subdue. At present they are largely obstreperous, rebellious, alienated, saying — " We will not have this man to rule over us," but in the new light which has broken upon us, we see that all these kingdoms of life belong potentially to God, and that it is the aim of the Christian religion to bring them into glad subjection to the King. The city of God is no longer a distant goal in the clouds to be reached after this life is over, it is rather a city which is to be brought down out of heaven, and given a place on the earth by the prayers and labors of men. The old prayer, " Thy Kingdom come, thy will be done on earth as it is done in heaven," is being prayed with a new meaning by tens of thousands of Christians, and we are no longer singing with the gusto of our fathers such hymns as those of Isaac Watts: " When I can read my title clear to mansions in the skies," but we rather turn to hymns like this: " The Son of God goes forth to war, a kingly crown to gain," and our hearts beat fast at the thrilling question: " Who follows in his train?"

Good men and women are more and more thinking of the common good. They are interested in social welfare. They consecrate themselves to social service. The problems which evoke the liveliest interest to-day are all social: the Domestic, the Industrial, the Commercial, the Denominational, the International — all these are but phases of the huge social question to which thinking men are now giving their minds. It has come to our age with all the freshness of a new revelation that we are social creatures, that no man either lives or dies to himself, but that all men live only in society, that personality develops by its relationships, and that we are literally members of one another. The problem is how to live together in good will and mutual helpfulness, how to coöperate harmoniously for the attainment of worthy ends. All our great problems then, may fittingly be called peace problems. How can we bring husbands and wives, parents and children to live peaceably together, working harmoniously for the building of a beautiful and Christian home life? How can we induce labor and capital to live together in hearty good will, each side giving to the other that which is due? How can the Golden Rule be carried out in business? How can the principle of competition be so tempered and curbed by the principle of brotherliness that commercial rivals shall not strive to crush one another, converting the world of business into a field of slaughter? How can we bring the various branches of the Christian church closer together, so that they shall coöperate with increased efficiency in casting out demons, and performing the works of God? How can we heal society, distracted and torn by class prejudices and hatreds? How can we break down the barriers and fill up the chasms, and bring alienated groups of men into sweeter and more wholesome relations? But the greatest of all problems remains to be mentioned: How shall we get the nations of the earth to live together in peace?

How shall we abolish war? How shall we train the nations to live and work together like members of a family? How shall we establish not simply the brotherhood of man, but the brotherhood of nations?

In comparison with this problem all the other problems dwindle. It is not easy to create peace in a city or a commonwealth or a nation. To bring diverse classes of population into friendly relations, even though they live under the same flag, is a task which is immense. But to bring the fifty-seven nations of the earth into a life that shall be dominated by the sentiment of good will, this is indeed a task sufficient to tax the resources not only of all the good men now alive, but almost, one would think, of God himself. It is so great that some stagger back from it stunned and unnerved. It is apparently so impossible of solution that men even of faith often turn away from it with despondent faces. Our civic problems are vexing, our industrial problems are bewildering, our race problems within our own borders are appalling enough to make many hearts faint, but the international problem is the most tangled, most myriad-sided, most baffling, most overwhelming of all.

For that reason it is the most interesting, fascinating, thrilling, rewarding of all the subjects to which an American can set his mind. What is the greatest theme about which any man in our time can speak? International Peace. What is the most needed bit of work that a man in our day can perform? Work for the creation of a Christian spirit among the nations of the earth. What is the most urgent duty before the Church of Christ in the United States at the present hour? A Christian attitude toward war, and a wholehearted insistence that the principles of Jesus of Nazareth shall be the principles of statesmanship, and that nations as well as individuals shall foundation their life on love. Christianity and International Peace — that is my subject. I can conceive of none greater, none more inspiring, none more urgent.

It is to the young men and young women of

America that our most puzzling problems must be brought. Youth is the season when the pulse beat is strong, and when the heart is not easily made afraid. As men grow older, many of them lose something of the courage which they once had, and become less hopeful both for themselves and for mankind. Young men and women are by the will of God dreamers. Visions come to them of the heights that have never yet been scaled, and voices plead with them to attempt what has never yet been done. That is why Jesus of Nazareth called only young men to be his disciples. He rolled the world upon their shoulders, knowing that it was none too heavy for them to bear. The beloved disciple liked to write to young men, giving as one of his reasons the fact that they are strong. Yes, youth is strong in faith, in courage, in scorn of the entangling traditions and precedents by which humanity is held back. It is not afraid to attack fortresses which have never fallen, to venture out upon uncharted seas, to dare attempt a beautiful and original achievement. America has been often praised for her idealism. We have many sins, but even our harshest critics have given us credit for an idealism which is refreshing and at times sublime. Will not our idealism rise to the demands of the present crisis? To what section of American youth has the world a better right to turn than to the students in our universities and colleges? Is it too much to say that America has thus far been disappointed on the whole in her college graduates? It was one of the dreams of our fathers that education would save us from the evils by which the old world had been afflicted. They hated ignorance and superstition, and at tremendous sacrifices, wherever they built a church, they also built a school. Even in the earliest days, in the midst of poverty, they laid the foundations of colleges in which their sons might be trained for the task of building a nation which should do God's will. Through nearly three hundred years, our country has been faithful to the dreams of its founders, and nowhere on the earth has money been poured out with such lavish generosity for educational equipment as under our flag. Our educational institutions have been our pride and glory. But, alas, they have not done what was so confidently expected. College graduates, in appalling numbers, walk in the ways of the ungodly, and stand in the way of sinners, and sit in the seat of the scornful. This last occupation is exceedingly common. Four years in college convert some men into confirmed critics. Unwilling to do anything heroic themselves, they sneer at those who are sacrificing themselves for the public good, and smile superciliously at the efforts of men the latchet of whose shoes they are not worthy to unloose. Some of the most dangerous men in our country are college graduates. Their intellectual equipment renders them doubly dangerous, for it gives them added power to carry out their schemes. Selfishness in possession of disciplined powers becomes sevenfold more a peril. Not a few of the men who have done most within the last fifty years to corrupt legislation, and to thwart the will of the people, and to bring law into disrepute, have been college men. One is constantly amazed at the lack of moral enthusiasm and spiritual vision of multitudes of the men who come out of our institutions of learning. How many colleges in the country, do you think, are alive to the tremendous importance of the problem of International Peace? How many University Presidents have given it their attention, and fitted themselves to become leaders in the thought of the world concerning it? How many of the Professors and Educational leaders of Europe have been awake on this subject through the last forty years? One would suppose that university teachers, men who are versed in history and all branches of learning, and who have sat at the feet of the sages of the centuries, would give attention to the sovereign problems of life, and not allow the poor world to go on staggering under burdens which are crushing, only at last to tumble into a ditch. What avails a knowledge of chemistry or biology or astronomy or language or mathematics, if the mind is left ignorant of the great laws of God by which humanity is governed, and if the heart is left dull to the movement of God's spirit in widening and elevating the thoughts of men? Shame on the college professor who wraps himself up in his little specialty, paying no attention to the world's problems. And shame on the college student who does not look beyond the athletic field into the heart of the great struggle in which mankind is engaged. Our large cities would never have disgraced us by their political corruption if our college men in greater numbers had gone into politics and done their full duty as citizens. The world would not be, to-day, in its deplorable plight if educated men in every country had trained themselves to take a deeper interest in public affairs, and to discipline their hearts to Christian ways of feeling toward foreign nations. Every college man owes it to himself and to his country to build up in himself an international mind, and to cultivate an international heart. What is the supreme end of a college? To train up Christian citizens of the world.

The discussion of this international problem just now is peculiarly opportune. It is easier than it has ever been to think outside of national boundaries. Ordinarily we are interested solely in our city, once or twice a year we get interested in our commonwealth, once in four years we give furious thought for a few days to national affairs. Many persons never get interested in foreign nations at all. But we are being trained. Recent events have broken down our narrow walls, and we have been compelled to think of other nations than our own. The map of the world has been unrolled before us. We have been obliged to take daily lessons in geography. We have studied not only the whole of Europe, but the distant East. A thousand facts of which we had been ignorant, have been impressed upon our mind. A new sort of book has found its way into our hands. We have been reading about nations which heretofore had failed to interest us. We have made the acquaintance of distinguished men who were complete strangers to us before last August. Our con-

versation has widened. Our thoughts have
ranged through wider spaces. New sets of
problems have been forced upon us. We cannot keep our mind from crossing the sea. We
cannot hold our hearts from hovering over
countries for which we formerly cared little.
We are sensitive now to every sound and sight
from abroad. Now is the time to think
soberly about our nation and its mission to the
world, our churches and their obligations to
mankind. The war has prepared our minds
to take in a colossal theme. It has predis-
posed us to pursue lines of thought which run
to the end of the world. We see many things
more clearly than we saw them six months
ago. We see them now in the glare of a great
conflagration. The gleam of that fire will
flash through the paragraphs of these lectures.
While you are listening to my voice you will
hear the groans of men, and the sobs of women
across the sea. While I speak of peace, you
will feel the horror of the European tragedy.
Our hearts are awed and sensitized by the fact
that we stand on the edge of an abyss of tears

and blood. The agony of Europe gives intensity to our desire to find out, if possible, how a similar calamity may be avoided. The impotency of the European church in the hour of need admonishes us to investigate the condition of American Christianity, and makes us more eager, I hope, to bring our churches more fully into line with the great purposes of God. He that hath ears will hear what the Spirit is saying through this heart-breaking experience of Europe to the churches and nations.

We are living in a new world. Columbus in the fifteenth century discovered a world which historians call new, but that world was not so new as the one in which we now live. America is newer now than it was in 1492. What America was in 1492 it had been for centuries. The whole world has been transformed within the last hundred years. There is a situation now which never existed before. There is a set of conditions to-day of which men of preceding generations knew nothing. Steam and electricity are the twin magicians which have made all things new. They have annihilated space. They have tunneled the mountains, and narrowed the seas. The ancient walls are all down. There are no hermit nations. Around the planet there is nothing but open doors. The continents have been linked together, first by electric wires, and now by the more subtle wires of the ether. We can see around the world and hear around it. What is done in one country is seen by all, what is whispered in one capital is published in all the other capitals. This annihilation of space has brought all the races for the first time in history face to face with one another. The nations all are neighbors. A thousand new points of contact have been established, every point of contact a possible source of friction. Traders go everywhere. Every nation is represented in every market of the world. The oceans are so many highways along which the nations drive their chariots in quest of pleasure and of gold. The world is now a city, the various nations are so many city wards. The streets are crowded with representatives of all kindreds and tribes and breeds. Science has made the earth a neighborhood. The neighborhood can never be destroyed. Nations can never go back into their former isolation. Races can never again hide themselves behind mountains or seas. For richer, for poorer, for better, for worse, all the nations must live together until death overtakes the world. The neighborhood is here. The problem is how to convert it into a brotherhood. That is the supreme task of the Christian religion; that is the cardinal problem of the twentieth century.

The sudden coming together of a crowd of nations and races is fraught with enormous peril. You cannot bring together a few hundred individuals in a mining camp without running the risk of disturbance, and lawlessness and bloodshed. How can you expect to bring huge masses of men known as nations close together, each one exercising the liberty to do what is right in its own eyes, without creating the possibility of all sorts of complications and disorders? The variety of races is itself a source of danger. The different grades of culture represented in these races give rise to misunderstandings and resentments. Their varied ambitions and ideals clash and create irritation. Each nation had become set in its own ways before the dividing walls were thrown down, and to get accustomed to strange manners, and to bear with equanimity curious customs is not easy. Differences of color of the skin, and differences of social ideals, and differences of manners are certain to give offense, but these differences cannot be at once annihilated. Races must get on with one another in spite of their disagreeable peculiarities and their estranging traditions.

Moreover, the past is not blotted out because it lies behind us. It is always influencing the present. Nations have had quarrels in former days, and the memories of those quarrels are vivid. Injustices have been done, and they are not forgotten. Wrongs have been perpetrated, and they are all remembered.

Harsh and cutting words have been spoken, and they rankle in the heart. Animosities float in the blood often down to the third and fourth generation. All the nations possess clashing tendencies and habits, and not a few of them are weighted with inherited jealousies and hatreds. There is abundant material for a great fire, for each nation contributes a bundle of fagots.

Modern science by bringing the nations together has released forces which are working mightily for mischief as well as for good. Men have now enlarged opportunities for making money. It is the age of the merchant. Commerce has taken on new dignity and volume. The merchant has a place in all the world's Parliaments, in several countries he can become the head of the state. But money making is a feverish enterprise. Trade develops in thousands of men a covetousness which knows no bounds. Competition for the great prizes becomes furious, and men often resort to methods which are unscrupulous and to tricks which are base. Along with the inherited animosities, we must reckon, then, commercial rivalries as perilous factors in the life of our modern world. The promoter is everywhere. He goes from country to country seeking concessions and privileges. He gets his clutches on gold mines and oil wells and railroads. He stakes off acres under foreign flags as a part of his desired possessions. The diplomats later on meet and discuss what they call spheres of influence. Each diplomat has at his back a nation provided with soldiers and guns. Weak nations succumb to the strong. Helpless populations are exploited for the advantage of capitalists far away. Commerce sometimes leads to peace, and sometimes it leads to war. Which one it leads to depends on the character of the men who are engaged in it. When commerce is carried on by ruffians and bullies, then commerce leads ultimately to war. There are many ruffians and bullies in the commercial world, and they have caused a deal of trouble. Corporations and syndicates of rich men invest their capital in foreign countries whose population is ignorant, and whose government is weak, and, by and by, on the occurrence of some slight misunderstanding or the perpetration of some insult or injustice, these rich men cry out for the use of the army and navy, demanding that their commercial investments shall be safeguarded by the blood of the sons of other men. Men now alive have seen a whole continent — Africa — carved up and distributed among the prominent nations of Europe. A part of Asia has been subjected to the same treatment. It has been counted desirable that a nation should have colonies, or dependencies. National pride has been stimulated by lofty talk of " possessions." Slavery being no longer fashionable, Christian nations now content themselves with owning what they call " inferior " populations, giving these populations what in the judgment of the owner is convenient and profitable for them. In the international world the strong has been preying on the weak, and diplomacy has been ranked according to its success in getting the advantage over other countries.

The diplomacy of the modern world has been largely Pagan. Diplomats are in general clever men learned in the art of getting the better of their rivals. Conduct that is counted contemptible among individuals is extolled as brilliant in ambassadors and diplomats. Lying and bullying and underhanded dealing have for a long time been common in the world of international business. The treatment of equal nations has been often dishonorable, the treatment of inferior nations has sometimes been atrocious. Statesmen have made a distinction between personal morality and national morality. They have believed that nations have a right to do that which is forbidden to individuals. It has been openly taught that principles of truth and honor which are binding on men in their social and commercial dealings are not binding on governments. In short, the international world has never been moralized. It is a part of the promised land which has not yet been subdued. Barbaric standards have been allowed to remain. The ideas of the cave man have in many places survived to the present hour.

It is because of the survival of these primitive ideas that we have also the survival of one of the practices of the primeval world — war, the custom of settling international questions by killing men. War belongs to a low stage of human development. It has no rightful place in the civilization of to-day. It is an anachronism, a nuisance, and a scandal. There are individuals who yet see in it something glorious, but they are men of stunted moral development. Men who are truly civilized look upon it with horror and loathing. Owing, however, to the low ideals of diplomacy it has been deemed necessary to perpetuate what is known as the policy of the big stick. The policy of the big stick is the policy of the brigand and rowdy. The big stick is an enormous army and a colossal navy. These are counted insignia of power. The Christian nations have for years spent a large amount of all their income upon these implements of blood. That educated men, and especially educated Christian men, have not cried out day and night against this, is one of the darkest tragedies of history.

The presence of these huge armaments complicates the situation, and renders the international problem still more baffling. For armaments create fear and fear breeds hate, and hate disturbs the normal working of the mind. All European life has for a generation been abnormal because of the enormous mass of steel and explosives piled up in readiness for a coming war. The human heart degenerates in the atmosphere impregnated by the poison of the barracks. National ideals go down whenever militaristic ideals go up. There has been for years a steady deterioration in the spiritual life of all the so-called great powers, and the church has not been able to check the fatal process. Militarism hangs like a millstone around the neck of the modern world. It is an octopus in whose huge tentacles the nations are tenaciously gripped. How to break the power of this octopus is one of the questions which every man of sense and grit must face. Until the world can check the advance of the militaristic idea, and overthrow the leaders who have been poisoned and demoralized by the militaristic ideal, there is little chance of bringing mankind up to a level where, clothed and in its right mind, it can deal rationally with the great tasks which modern civilization has given it to do.

America is one of the world powers, and nothing is foreign to the United States which touches the higher interests of humanity. We cannot even if we would lead a life of national isolation. We are bound up in a thousand ways with the interests of the world. Our goods go to every market. Every country contributes to our necessities and comfort. Our inventions are used in every land. Our ideas are reported around the globe. Our books are read wherever men have minds to think. It is not necessary for us to make entangling alliances, they make themselves. Our merchants make them, our travelers, our missionaries, our scientists and scholars and inventors.   We are already knit to all the nations of the earth.   We cannot keep ourselves at home, nor can we keep the outside world from flowing in upon us.   The weight of our opinion is greater than we know.   The power of our example is more potent than it is possible for us to measure.   We know that within the last six months every nation engaged in war has shown a regard for our opinion, and that several of them have put forth strenuous efforts to secure our favorable judgment on their conduct.   Rulers as well as statesmen have laid their case before the people of the United States as before a tribunal whose decision is of weight and worth.   What we think and do is of moment in the making of the world.   The man who helps to mold America is helping to shape the destiny of all mankind. If we can make our great republic a steadfast and implacable hater of war and a faithful and indefatigable worker for peace, we shall have hastened the coming of the day when war shall be no more.   We have never begun to do yet what it is in the mind of God we shall do.

We are as yet only a baby nation. No one has ever suggested that we are decadent. No one imagines that we have passed the zenith of our glory. Our day has only well begun. Our career is still before us. We have not yet put forth our strength. If we use the powers which heaven has given us we can mold and guide the world. We should, therefore, pay heed to our attitude, conscious of its ultimate possible consequences. We do not live in a corner, and we cannot do our work unobserved. There was a time when wide oceans separated us from the rest of the world, but now they are bonds which unite us. Instead of being barriers, they are broad avenues upon which the nations come flocking to our doors.

This world peace problem belongs to the whole American people, but it is especially a problem for the Christian church. The church is free here in a sense in which it is not free in many lands. Our church is not allied with the state, and hence it is not handicapped by state policy or traditions. Our ministers are not paid by the government, and hence are not tempted to echo the opinion of governmental officials. The leaders of religion here can strike false ideas and policies as hard as they will, and can boldly discuss problems from which their ministerial brethren in foreign lands must studiously hold aloof.

There is no question now before the world in which the future of Christianity is so vitally involved as this question of international peace. The church cannot survive if militarism is to rule. Christianity must languish if Cæsar is to sit on the throne. A house divided against itself cannot stand. A nation cannot have the ideals of Christ permanently in its homes, if it enthrones the ideals of Cæsar in the capitol. We cannot successfully teach the boys the Golden Rule if diplomats are lauded for ignoring it. We cannot sing hymns to the God of love, if the money of the people is being progressively squandered in the manufacture of instruments of destruction. We cannot get men to look adoringly upon Jesus dying on the cross, when the magazines and papers are filled with pictures of battleships, and battalions of soldiers drilling for the work of human slaughter. Christianity and militarism are implacable and deadly foes. You cannot serve them both, you will come at last to hate the one and love the other, or you will cling to the one and despise the other.

National policy, then, is within the range of legitimate pulpit instruction. Those who would silence the preachers of the gospel on international problems are silencing the witnesses of Christ on the very themes on which their testimony is most needed. It was on national policy that the Hebrew prophets spoke in tones of thunder. All the politicians of Jerusalem combined could not close the mouth of Isaiah or Jeremiah. No doubt many a good soul in those ancient times wished the prophets would content themselves with pious meditations on the goodness of Jehovah, but the prophets knew that it is in its national policy that a nation's deepest life expresses

itself, and that it is what a nation says by its
example rather than by what individuals say
by their precepts that the character of young
men is molded and the destiny of the nation
determined.   The American pulpit is recreant
to its highest trust if it does not insist in season and out of season upon the introduction
of Christian principles in national policies,
and if it does not demand that the attitude of
our nation to all other nations shall be that
of a Christian man to his brothers.   To allow
militarists to go on week after week educating
by their articles in magazines and Sunday papers the boys and young men of the nation
while the pulpit is silent on the greatest of
all public questions, is sheer madness.   Ministers of Christ cease to be either light or salt
the moment they confine themselves to a few
platitudinous commonplaces which everybody
believes already, and against which no one
can offer a word of objection, leaving untouched the burning moral questions in which
the very life and destiny of the nation are
involved.

But it is not only the preachers who must work, the laymen also must gird up their loins. This is a herculean task, and every man is needed. It is a task which concerns more than the Christian church. We must have the assistance of the Jews, and of the agnostics, and the infidels, and of the great unchurched masses. Every one who has in him a desire to better humanity, and a willingness to assist in casting out one of the most ancient and furious of all the devils, should be welcomed. Few have any conception of the magnitude and difficulty of the task. Militarism has a grip upon Europe so tenacious that if one did not believe in the existence of a God of love, who is also omnipotent, one might well despair of victory. There are groups of men in our own country so obsessed by the militarist ideal and so astute in their methods of working that they have within the last thirty years been able in spite of our inherited traditions and temper to push their schemes one after another through the national congress and to poison by their writings and speeches the minds and hearts of millions. It is not enough to want peace, or to admire peace or to pray for peace. We must work for peace. We must make it. Like all other fine things it is the result of the forthputting of effort. It can come only by the sweat of brain and the agony of heart. The world could have had peace long ago, if only men had been willing to pay the price for it. Like all the best things it comes by way of the cross — by way of self-sacrificing love. Jesus pronounced no beatitude on the peace wishers, or peace dreamers, or peace praisers, or peace hopers, but only on the peace makers, the men who establish the foundations of justice and good will by the energetic exercise of all the powers of their soul.

It is common in certain circles to believe that everything is coming out right, no matter what we do. The law of evolution is in full force, men feel, and the universe is so made that it will unfold after the fashion of a rose. No matter what we think or say or do, to-morrow is certain to be better than to-day. This is the good old comfortable doctrine of Laissez faire. " Let things alone. Keep your hands off. Permit things to go how they will." It is a false doctrine. That is not the way to bring peace. The nations will never come into a brotherhood if brotherly hearted men fold their arms and wait for them to come. Brotherly hearted men must breathe their spirit into the public mind, and into public policy. Those who believe in brotherhood must drive from the seats of power men of a different temper. False ideals must be torn down. Mistaken notions must be rooted out of the mind. Organizations created for the purpose of catering to ambition and greed and vanity must be resisted and overthrown. New institutions must be created through which the world's better self can express itself. New legislation must be enacted by which the heart's dreams can be fulfilled. The world must be reshaped by hands made strong because they have been held in the hands that were pierced. Militarism is the arch devil of the modern world. Do you think it can be cast out by a few hopes and wishes — a few prayers and speeches? I tell you Nay! It can be cast out only by the agony and sweat of tens of thousands of men who have determined that by God's grace they will never give up until the victory has been won.

The first thing is to take hold of the work. Get a good grip upon it and never let it slip out of your hands. Let the scoffers say what they will, but go on with your work — Be patient. Victory is not coming to-day nor to-morrow nor the day after. It may not come in your lifetime. No matter. Work till the sun goes down and the night falls in which you cannot work any more, and some one, noting your fidelity, will take up the work where you dropped it, and then another, and then still another, and some day, somehow, the glorious triumph will be complete.

Many peace workers are just now discouraged. This is foolish. There are convulsions in human history just as there are in nature, but geology assures us that the convulsions never thwarted the onward and upward movement of the earth. The convulsions in human history may shatter empires and paralyze civilizations, but mankind will not be destroyed. Mankind may slip back. It has slipped back at times, and it will no doubt slip back again. There is such a thing, the evolutionists tell us, as arrested development and degeneration, and we must expect these things in the history of our race. But while nations may degenerate, and whole races may drop from the tree of life, humanity will move onward, for the Lord God Almighty is with those who fear him. Let us feast our hearts upon the light which by the eye of faith we can see over the tops of the coming years. Let us not ever be weary in well doing, for in due season we shall certainly reap if we do not faint.

Have you ever asked of yourself soberly, What is the mission of our Republic? What is the errand on which it has been sent? What is the word which it has been ordained to speak to all the nations of the earth? What is the particular task to which it has been set apart? What is the function which in the divine intention it was created to fulfill? Sometimes we have been told that America's mission is the establishment of freedom. It is liberty, exalted by us, which is going to enlighten the world. The Republic was founded by Washington and saved by Lincoln — so men say — in order that the scepter of tyranny might be broken, and the rights of the people to life and liberty and the pursuit of happiness might be enthroned. But liberty is not an end. Liberty is a means. Liberty is not the goal. Liberty is a way station on the road which leads to the goal. Liberty is a condition under which human life can be developed. The final word in the vocabulary of life is not liberty, but love. Love is the fulfilling of the law. Love is the greatest thing in the world. The kingdom of love is the goal. To establish the reign of love is the sublimest of all achievements, and may it not be that this is the very work to which our Republic has been specially called? The ideal which Christianity holds before us is the king-

dom of God — the kingdom of righteousness
and peace and joy. Sometimes the kingdom
is represented as a city, and the nations of
the earth are pictured carrying their wealth
into it. The kingdom of God as the New
Testament conceives it is not a contracted
kingdom, but one which is as wide as the
world. All the nations are to be incorporated
in it, and to win them to allegiance to its heavenly ideals is the highest of all privileges and
duties. Is this your ideal of American greatness? Is this the destiny we are to carve?
Is this the purpose of our national existence?
To assist the burdened and weary hearted nations toward the shining goal — the kingdom
of God — the kingdom of Righteousness and
Peace and Joy?

It is as an American, then, that I speak to
you, Americans, about what we owe to our
country. We certainly owe it the best that
is in us, expended in a lifelong endeavor to
make our country what it ought to be, what
God wants it to be, and what by his grace and
our consent it will be. It is as an American

Christian that I speak to you, American Christians, about what we owe to Jesus Christ our Savior. We certainly owe him the best that is in us expended in a lifelong effort to build up in our Republic the kingdom of love in order that through its example, the kingdom of love may be finally established throughout the world.

It was just twenty years ago that, after a hundred days in Europe, I reached the conclusion that in the world of my generation the supreme problem was that of international peace. Once convinced that the peace movement was the most important of all movements, I consecrated to it all my powers for the remainder of my life. For twenty years I have carried the burden on my heart, constantly asking myself what further thing the Christian church can do in order to quicken interest in this subject and to hasten the day when a lasting peace can be established among the nations of the earth. By study and travel and reflection, I have endeavored to acquaint myself with the dimensions of the problem.

In every country of Europe I have pondered it. In many commonwealths of our own country I have spoken of it. And now I lay the subject before you. Some of you have thought about it already. I trust you will think about it more. Others of you have never given it serious attention. Perhaps something I shall say may create in you a deepened interest. I want to hold the subject before you until it burns itself into your heart and conscience. I desire to unfold it, and spread it out, and illustrate it until you shall see clearly how vast and far reaching it is. I desire to light it up, if I can, so that whatever confusion may be lurking in your minds may be so far as possible dissipated. I cannot exhaust the theme in six lectures. I can call your attention only to a few aspects of the myriad-sided problem. It is an economic question — all political economists ought to be interested in it. It is a business question — all financiers and merchants ought to study it. It is an industrial question. All wage earners and labor leaders ought to investigate it. It is a political question — all who are interested in the science and art of government ought to give it prolonged attention. It is a philanthropic question — all lovers of mankind ought to be drawn to it. It is a moral question — all students of ethics ought to think out the numerous puzzling questions which spring out of it. But it is fundamentally a religious question. It involves our conception of God and our relation to him, and our relation to our fellowmen, and all who are striving to keep a conscience void of offense toward God and toward man should invoke the illumination of the Holy Spirit that their minds may be guided to conclusions which will be in harmony with the mind of their Creator. No matter what one's creed or calling or position, he ought to study the question with earnestness and patience, for it is a question which touches the happiness and welfare not only of millions now alive, but of unnumbered generations yet unborn. To no one, however, so much as to the Christian, does the question come with urgent and unescapable power, for to the Christian, Jesus Christ is the Prince of Peace, and to make Christ regnant in the affairs of men is the deep desire of every truly Christian heart.   How to enthrone this Prince in the vast and troubled realm of international life in our turbulent and tempestuous century, is not only the most important, but also the most difficult of all the problems with which men and women of brain and heart and conscience have to deal.

II

The Bible and War

WHAT has the Bible to say about war?
The question is forced upon us by what is
going on in Europe. Men are asking the question to-day who never asked it before. Many
are searching the Scriptures for light in the
present distress. For the war is in that quarter of the world where the influence of the
Bible has been longest at work. All the nations in the great war except two have for
centuries claimed to find in the Bible the re-
vealed character and will of God. It is chiefly
Christians who are killing one another. The
armies are made up of men who have had no
sacred book except the Bible. It is time we
were asking ourselves what is the attitude of
the Bible to war?

It is an interesting fact that for many a

century the war makers and peace makers have quoted the Bible in their support. Seldom has a war been waged in which its leaders did not appeal to the Bible. Generals and private soldiers alike have fed their hearts in hours of darkness and peril out of the same big book. What Cromwell did in the seventeenth century, and the American revolutionist in the eighteenth, and Paul Kruger in the nineteenth, the Emperor of Germany is doing in the twentieth. Wars are carried on under the avowed sanction of the God who inspired the Bible. On the other hand, all the opponents of war have made a constant appeal to the same book. Texts have been quoted a thousand times to prove that war is an abomination absolutely contrary to the will of God. Thousands of peacemakers are heartened in their labors by what is said in the Book of books. They fortify themselves behind words of prophets and apostles. They quote the declarations of the Prince of Peace. The militarist and the pacifist alike turn to the Scriptures for ap-

proval of the courses which they pursue. How can we account for this singular phenomenon?

When we open the Old Testament and begin to glance through its pages, it seems to be largely a history of wars. The chosen people are always fighting, and they fight under the guidance and protection of their God, Jehovah. It is he who goes before them into battle, who fights with them in all their struggles, and who gives them the victory. He himself is a man of war, he is a God of battles. And the men who wrote about these wars are apparently not at all shocked by the atrocities and barbarities which they record. Massacres and wars of extermination are not condemned, but on the other hand commended as being parts of the great plan of Jehovah. The historians of the early history of Israel have no words of condemnation for even the savagery of warfare, and accept it as a form of religious activity. Even the prophets sometimes saw the future only through the ideals of a world ruled by force. One of them saw the Messiah seated on a throne and ruling with a rod of iron, having dominion from sea to sea. Many of the poets of Israel also are stirred to enthusiasm by the martial spirit. They sing with gusto of martial deeds. They put crowns of laurel on the brows of military leaders. They ascribe military powers to Jehovah. It is by his favor that the enemy is overthrown. One of them sings:

> " He teacheth my hands to war
>   So that my arms do bend a bow of brass.
>   Thou hast girded me with strength unto the battle,
>   Thou hast subdued under me those that rose up
>   against me."

Another one blesses Jehovah as the one

> " Who teacheth my hands to war
>   And my fingers to fight."

The Old Testament extols David above all the Hebrew kings, a man after God's own heart, and David was the nation's favorite military chieftain. It was he who taught the children of Israel the song of the bow, and who sang:

> " By thee I run upon a troop,
>   By my God do I leap over a wall."

Not a few then of the religious leaders and teachers of Israel apparently exult in the paraphernalia and victories of war. Military language comes readily to their lips, and they picture history in the imagery of battle.

But in the Old Testament there are other and higher voices, voices which have in them the piercing tone of a great lament, which burn with the passion of a fierce condemnation, and which thrill with the expectation of a reign of peace. There were men in Israel who did not delight in thinking of God as a man of war or as one mighty in battle, but who loved to think of him as a great benefactor and giver of peace. One of them spoke of a day when Jehovah was going to break the bow and the sword and the battle out of the land, and make his people lie down in safety. Another saw a huge bonfire in which the boots of war and the garments rolled in blood were to be consumed. Visions of a golden age kept flitting before the eyes of the greatest of these preachers, and in that golden age war had ceased to be. Its devastations and tragedies were ended.   The instruments of slaughter were all converted into the implements of industry, and nations no longer lifted up sword against each other, neither did they practice the art of warfare any more.   The greatest of all the prophets saw that the golden age would be created by a mighty personality, a myriad sided man, a hero with many gifts, a king with many crowns, a lord with many titles, and the proudest of his titles would be " Prince of Peace."   If the Psalm book is full of military feeling, it is also full of the feeling that stirs in the hearts of those who hate the sights and sounds of war.   Some of the sweet singers of Israel were always sneering at the horse. In Palestine the horse was used only in war. He became the symbol of military preparedness and power.   There were Israelites who believed that a nation's strength lies in its military equipment, there were others who held the opposite opinion.   Listen to the poet who says:

" There is no king saved by the multitude of a host.
    A horse is a vain thing for safety."

There were men then as there are men now who were deeply impressed by the discipline and physical development which the army gives, and there were others who looked upon all this as foolishness.   Listen to this outbreak of disgust:

" He delighteth not in the strength of the horse;
    He taketh not pleasure in the legs of a man."

Whom does the Lord, then, take pleasure in? The poet answers:

" The Lord taketh pleasure in them that fear him,
    in those that hope in his mercy."

Here then in the Old Testament we find contradictory voices.   The men who wrote the Bible did not agree in their estimate of war. Their attitudes to it were not the same.   They differed in their opinions and feelings as men do now.   It is interesting to see how vividly and variously they disagreed.   It is because the Bible is such a many sided and frank and unconventional book that it is capable of monstrous abuse.   No other book in the world has been so misused as the Bible. That misuse continues to the present hour. You can prove anything you wish by snatching isolated sentences from the Bible. Men are doing now what they did in the days of Shakespeare — they are quoting Scripture to uphold their favorite theories. In hot scorn the great poet wrote:

"What damned error but some sober brow to bless it,
  And approve it with a text?"

We are not prepared to deal fairly with the Bible until we see that it is not one book, but a library of sixty-six books, written by different men, with different temperaments and different viewpoints, and different measures of wisdom, and different degrees of spiritual vision, at different times, amid different circumstances, to meet different needs, the times being scattered over a period of at least fifteen hundred years. The Bible is the sifted literature of a gifted people, a people more splendidly endowed religiously than any other people known to history. But like all other races the Jews were under the law of development. They grew. They advanced in wisdom. Their thoughts were widened with the process of the suns. Their heart and conscience were refined and instructed by the experiences of the centuries. Their great men were not equal. Great personalities are of different types. It takes many kinds of men to mould a nation or lead a world. What a variety of character and talent and virtue you find in the company of heroes and heroines who pass before us in the eleventh chapter of the letter to the Hebrews. The Old Testament is the record of the development of a wonderful people which reached conceptions of God and man and duty and destiny which have had an immeasurable influence upon the character and career of a large part of the human race. When you therefore ask: What does the Bible say about war? you are asking a question more difficult to answer than you think. It does not say any one thing, it says many things, and different things, and you must discriminate among these various things and decide which one of them is the highest, and which you can accept as God's voice to you. There are low voices and high voices in the Scriptures, for men live always at different levels, and we are to listen ever to the highest. Now the highest voice in the Bible is not in the Old Testament at all. The Old Testament was the Bible of the Jewish church, the New Testament is the Bible of Christians. We retain the Jewish Bible because it has in it much that is valuable and which humanity cannot afford to ignore or disparage. The Christian church is richer because the Old Testament is bound up together with the New. But in this union there is a danger against which we must always be on our guard. The two Testaments are not on the same level. They are not equal authorities for our life. We are Christians, and when we lift up our eyes in search of one who shall speak with authority, we see no man but Jesus only. We cannot go to Moses or to David, to Joshua or to Solomon for the final word to guide us through our difficulties.

There is no one to whom we can go but Jesus, for he alone has the words of eternal life. What Hebrew law-makers and priests thought and said of war centuries ago has no more significance for us than what they said about slavery and polygamy, and a hundred other matters. They cannot lay down rules for us. They cannot be our teachers in the tangled problems of our modern world. The time will never come when men will not get suggestion, stimulus, and inspiration from the Hebrew scriptures, but as soon as the Old Testament is used as an authoritative statute book for us, it becomes a millstone around the neck of the Christian church, and holds it back from doing the work of Christ. We cannot wisely listen to any man but Jesus. He is the great teacher. He is the way, the truth, the life. He warns us not to listen to the men of the early times. "It was said by them of old time, thou shalt do thus and thus, but I say unto you, thou shalt do just the opposite." The people were astonished at this teaching, remarking that he taught as one possessing authority and not as the Scribes. The Scribes were adepts in quotation, experts in collecting precedents, sticklers for tradition, pedants who had put out their eyes by studying manuscripts handed down from ages whose ethical ideals had been outgrown.

The misuse of the Old Testament is responsible for the perpetuation of more than one abomination. It has furnished proof texts for Mormonism, and it bolstered up the cause of the slaveholder, and it has often fed the flames of war. When used by ignorance, or by superstition, or by fanaticism, it is one of the most dangerous books in all the world.

Let us then open our New Testament, and find out if we can what is the attitude of our Christian Bible to war. Here we meet with a chilling disappointment. To our amazement the New Testament has nothing to say about war. It does not commend it, or condemn it. It is silent on the whole subject. It passes it by as though it were a theme of no interest. Not one of the New Testament writers cares to discuss it. Not one of the apostles ever expressed an opinion concerning it. Even St. Paul, always versatile and alert and courageous, leaves this topic alone. But surely the Master will not allow us to go uninformed in a matter so momentous. He will tell us fully what lies in his own heart. Alas, he does not. Strange to say, the apostles never attempted to draw out his mind on this subject. They asked him many questions, but never, so far as we know, a question about war. Has physical force a legitimate place in the business of society and nations? Is physical resistance sometimes a duty? Is physical coercion of human beings ever a necessity? These are questions which men have been asking for centuries, and to none of them did Jesus give an answer. He insisted on the supremacy of the principle of love, but he never told the world whether in his judgment the use of physical force is at all times inconsistent with the love principle. Is it possible to love men and at the same time coerce them by physical means into courses which they would not if left to themselves take? There is no

question more important and more puzzling
in our modern world than — What is the
Christian attitude toward war? The Christian attitude is of course the Christ attitude,
but what is the Christ attitude? What attitude did Jesus of Nazareth take to the wars,
for instance, of the Maccabees? What did
he think of the argument which justifies wars
of defense? So far as the records go, he
never disparaged military service. He did
not suggest to the centurion that he was in a
vile business, and must at once abandon it.
In the gospels, the military officials are always
spoken of with high respect, and sometimes
with commendation. Jesus did not on any oc-
casion forbid nations waging war. No condemnation of war in specific terms can be
found in his teaching. Whether the use of
physical force in the maintenance or furtherance of moral ends is ever according to the
will of God, and whether the use of physical
compulsion is ever indispensable to the successful carrying out of the purposes of the
Eternal are large questions which he leaves

untouched. It is one of the bitterest of all the many disappointments which we meet with at the hands of the New Testament, that it maintains an unbroken silence on the ethics of war. When we lift up our eyes to the great Teacher and say: " Speak, Lord, for this problem troubles me, and thy servant waits for the decisive word," our appeal brings back no response, the lips of the Master are dumb.

What shall we say then? Shall we say that this is not a question for Christians to deal with? Shall we conclude that Christianity cares for none of these things? Shall we settle down in the conviction that to follow Jesus is to follow him in his silence as well as in his speech, and that with national questions we as Christians have nothing to do? If this is sound reasoning, then we must have nothing to say on questions of education, or business, or recreation, or politics, or art, or literature, or any other of the kingdoms in which the men of our day live, for about none of these did Jesus have a word to say. There is no evidence that any of them ever entered his mind.

If we are to ignore everything about which Jesus kept silent, we shall pass by a large part of all which the modern world counts important. We shall shake off our heaviest responsibilities, and shamefully shirk the most difficult and important of our duties. War is a large fact in our modern world, and it is our imperative duty to work out clear conceptions of it, and to take a Christian attitude toward it.

In helping us do this, we have two faithful and ever present guides: first, the recorded words of Jesus; and second, the Holy Spirit, who, being the spirit of Jesus, continues the work of Jesus, and guides his servants into all the truth.

While there are no words of Jesus specifically condemning war or dealing with the question of the legitimacy of the use of force, his words breathe the spirit of gentleness and persuasion. In his presence we breathe an atmosphere totally different from that of the camp of Cæsar. There is nothing to suggest the barracks or the battlefield. He carries us at once into a different world, and sets us in the midst of a different set of forces. There is not a hint of compulsion or a glorification of physical power. For instance, " Blessed are the meek, for they shall inherit the earth." It must have seemed a wild and visionary declaration, for the arrogant and imperious had up to that time held in their grip the kingdoms of the world. " Blessed are the peacemakers, for they shall be called the sons of God." That smote as with a sword the universal sentiment of the ages. From time immemorial the war makers had been called the sons of deity. While alive, they had been idolized, and after death their marble figures on marble pedestals had held the veneration of succeeding generations. Blessed are the war makers, the battle chieftains, the conquerors, the pillagers and destroyers! For them and them alone had triumphal arches been erected, and their names alone bore a luster which the lapse of time did not dim. But now a Galilean peasant throws an idea into the human mind: " Blessed are the

peacemakers, for they shall be recognized as
the sons of the Highest." As for himself he
had no use for a sword. When one of his
disciples drew a sword in his defense, he
smote him with a swift rebuke. He refused
to defend himself against the Roman soldiers
who came to arrest him. He went unre-
sistingly to death, even the death of the cross.
He could have called legions of angels to fight
for him. He refused.

All his life he had extolled the peace-mak-
ing virtues, mercy, and kindness, and gentleness, and tenderness, and brotherliness, and
service, and constantly he had condemned the
motives which lead to war, envy and vanity
and ambition and greed and anger and suspicion and hatred. All the demons which
combine to kindle the flames of war were re-
buked by him and placed under an everlasting ban. His constant themes were the divine
fatherhood and the human brotherhood, and
he overarched the world with the idea that
men constitute one family, living in the
Father's house.

Does he condemn war? Not by name, but he condemns it. He condemns war just as he condemns slavery, and all other institutions which work havoc with the hearts and homes of men. It is his custom not to strike at the trunk or the branches, he lays the axe at the root of the tree. If he had picked out certain social and political evils and anathematized these, other evils would have sprung up after his death, no less mischievous and deadly, against which no words of his could have been quoted. He did not work with the multitudinous manifestations of the spirit of evil. He descended at once into the depths of the heart, knowing that it is only by a new heart that all the world's tragedies can be ended. His great words are, "Repent"—"change your mind," "you must be born again." Whoever preaches with power the doctrine of the Fatherhood of God and the brotherhood of man, is striking heavy blows at polygamy and slavery and war, and every other member of the direful brood of scourges by which mankind has been plagued.

But while the spirit of Jesus is in deadly conflict with the spirit of war, the question still remains as to what shall be our attitude when war comes. It must needs be that offenses come, as Jesus clearly confessed, and experience proves that among these inevitable offenses, war thus far is one. Social evils cannot be abolished by magic. Institutional abominations cannot be exorcised by the waving of the hand. Slavery, for instance, could not be abolished in the first century or the second or the third. It was a monstrous institution, but Christians were not numerous enough to overthrow it. They had to accommodate themselves to it, and get on with it as best they could. What cannot just now be cured must be endured until the happy hour arrives when cure is possible. Christianity has no power in this world except through the hearts which are surrendered to it, and its influence is therefore a progressive one, its power at any moment depending on the number of its adherents and the completeness of their surrender to its principles. Not enough

hearts have as yet been subdued by the spirit
of Jesus to banish war from our planet, and
since it survives, the question is, what shall
we think of it, what shall we say about it, how
shall we act? Shall we denounce all wars,
and condemn all armies which take part in
them? Shall we say that to fight in an army
is unchristian, and that every Christian who
marches to the battlefield is a traitor to Christ?
Shall we say that to shoot men on the battlefield is murder — a violation of the sixth commandment — and that to justify participation
in armed conflict is a repudiation of that which
is fundamental in the Christian religion?

It must be borne in mind that we are living
in a growing world. The human race is in
a process of evolution. The stages of this
evolution are tedious and protracted, and
many crudities and immaturities must be borne
with until the principle of progress has carried
us beyond them. War from the ideal stand-
point is of course monstrous. In a completed
world war could not be. When men have
reached their growth, they will be unable to

shoot one another down in battle. But robbery is also monstrous, and so is defalcation,
and so is forgery, and so is slander, and so is
drunkenness, and so are all the crimes which
appear in the docket of our civil courts. But
we have to deal with them. We cannot act
as though they did not exist. We must curb
them as much as we can. We do not seem to
be able to curb them without the use of force.
Experience proves that the use of force is
both salutary and indispensable. It will never
do to say, these things are too unsavory for
us to think about or handle, please let us think
always of the world as it ought to be. We
must use our reason and our conscience, and
all the powers of a discriminating judgment.

We must find out, therefore, if there be a
distinction in wars, and if it be possible for
men to go into war from different motives.
For instance, one man might go to war for
purposes of revenge, whereas another might
march against him for purposes of defend-
ing that which is too precious for the world
to lose. A man might enlist in an army which

was fighting for plunder, and another might become a soldier in a great campaign for liberation. Motive then is a factor in the problem which cannot be neglected, and belligerents are to be classified not by the character of their weapons, but by the motives which drive the contending armies to the field of blood.

But the stern question still confronts us: Is not war a sin in itself, and can any motive, however holy, justify one in participating in the commission of a sin?

We are dependent here entirely on the spirit of God; and his guidance, because of human infirmities, has not yet led all conscientious and faithful men to the same goal. There have been those in every Christian generation who have said that to resist evil by physical force is always unchristian. This is Tolstoi's position, and he presented it with such eloquence and persistency and courage that he made a profound impression on large classes of minds. The religion of Jesus was to Tolstoi very simple. It can be summed up under three heads: "Resist not evil, judge not, be not angry." So certain is he that this is the law of life that he is willing to obey it at any cost. He sweeps patriotism away. He abolishes the state. He will not allow civil law or tribunals or prisons. The whole system of government, and love of country must go, for otherwise you cannot get rid of war. There are many persons who feel that Tolstoi's interpretation of Christianity is the only honest one. All others are subterfuges and makeshifts and tricky evasions. It is often said that nobody to-day pretends to be a Christian in the New Testament sense, and that Christianity as taught by Christ is repudiated by all of his followers. Why? Because Christ says: "Resist not him that is evil." We all do. "Whosoever smiteth thee on thy right cheek, turn to him the other also." And none of us does this. "If any man would go to law with thee and take away thy coat, let him have thy cloak also." No one of us is willing to obey. "Whosoever shall compel thee to go one mile, go with him

twain." This also we refuse to do. "Give
to him that asketh thee, and from him that
would borrow of thee turn not thou away."
And yet we turn away from beggars every
day. Therefore we are not Christians. We
do not practice what we profess. We are
hypocrites, and the modern church is a sham.

It is a plausible indictment, but it ought
not to influence any one who has mastered
the elementary principles of New Testament
interpretation. Tolstoi was a man of genius,
and like many another genius, he was at times
near to madness. True to the habit of his
race, he was a literalist, incapable of properly
reading the metaphors of oriental speech.
Moreover, he was in everything an extremist,
reacting violently against his unfortunate en-
vironment. No one of us can understand the
conclusions of Tolstoi until we acquaint ourselves with the gigantic evils against which
he uttered his passionate protest. Patriotism
as he saw it was hateful, and so also was the
state. No wonder he longed for deliverance
from both of them. While we acknowledge

his extraordinary strength of personality and his amazing literary skill, we should never allow ourselves to be misled by his aberrations, or confused by his fanciful New Testament interpretations. In seizing upon one sentence and making that a universal rule of life, he committed the same sort of blunder committed by the mediæval monks who, reading that the Master told a certain rich young man to sell all that he had and give it to the poor, leaped to the conclusion that this is a law for everybody, and that only men who possess nothing are certain of admittance to heaven. Jesus never laid down rules. He dealt in principles alone. His fundamental principle is love. Whatever we do, we are to do it in subjection to that principle. For instance, we are not to give to a child all the candy that he asks for. We are to give only as love allows us to give. We must give for the child's good. We cannot give to the street beggar whose breath indicates the direction in which he will travel when the next coin is put into his hand. Love forbids

us to give to every one who asks, and we are
bound to be true to the law of love. We are
not to resist an evil man, unless the cause of
love demands it. Sometimes non-resistance
would prove a blessing to him, at other times
it might prove a curse. There are men who
are saved by being resisted. No man can
consistently maintain on the authority of the
teaching of Jesus the doctrine of non-resistance, unless he is prepared to advocate and
practice the habit of indiscriminate and universal giving. Any man in a large city who
gives to every one who asks, not only im-
poverishes himself, but works havoc upon the
community. Giving is certainly a sin when it
hurts the giver and the person given to and
the town. It is monstrous to say that such
giving is commanded by the Son of God.

When, therefore, men tell us that Christianity teaches the doctrine of non-resistance,
we must understand more fully what they
mean. The man who says that the use of
physical force is never justifiable either in
defense of life, or of a principle more valuable

to the world than life, is not aware of the reach of the words he is using. For instance, if a mad bull should rush at you in the field, you would at once use all the force in your possession to beat him back. And if an escaped lunatic should meet you in the street, imagining that he had been commanded by God to kill you, you would use force upon him as freely as upon a bull. And if, not a lunatic but a drunken man, having put an enemy into his mouth to steal away his brains, should attack you with a murderer's knife, would you doubt your right to beat him off with any weapon you could lay your hands on? And now if a man neither insane nor drunk, but simply wicked, a man with moral powers imperfectly developed, should at midnight attempt to force his way into your house, you would not count yourself a Pagan if you made use of force to put him out. If you could not do it yourself, you would call in the force of the policeman. There is a spirit in man, and the inspiration of the Almighty gives him understanding. We seem to know instinctively that we may properly use force at certain times and under certain circumstances even to save our own life. But when it comes to saving the life of others, our intuitions are still stronger and quicker. What strong man could see a bully trampling a little boy without rescuing him by the use of physical force, if he could not rescue him in any other way? Who could witness a ruffian threatening a girl or woman without coming at once to her defense? Who could lie still and allow a burglar to murder his wife and children, believing it wrong to resist evil? It is not written in any book that on such occasions we may use force, it is written on the tables of the heart. It is a law sacred and divine which antedates the decalogue, and it will never be repealed.

Now if there are times when the individual is justified in the use of force, it is likely that there will come times when the use of force by the community is necessary. Cities as well as men must occasionally use compulsion. It is difficult to see how the life of any

American city could go on without policemen
and courts, jails and sheriffs. Would it be a
good thing for the thieves and the thugs if
all the policemen should lay down their night-
sticks? Would it be just to the decent people of a community to allow the desperadoes
and cut-throats to lord it over them? That
a city has a right to use force is among all
practical men considered axiomatic. Civilization, as we know it, would fall into chaos were
all the instruments and machinery of force re-
moved. As Paul said: " The ruler is the
minister of God to thee for good. But if
thou do that which is evil, be afraid; for he
beareth not the sword in vain: for he is the
minister of God, a revenger to execute wrath
upon him that doeth evil."

Now if a city is justified in the employment of force, who can deny the same right
to a nation? A nation is only a larger social
group, and if a small group has the right to
protect itself from evildoers, a large group
must possess this right also. Lunatics,
drunken men, robbers, may break in, and

a nation has the right to self protection.
But its right runs further. The right
to save others is a loftier right than that of
saving one's self. If a strong man is justified in going to the defense of a man who is
weak, then a strong nation may give a weak
nation assistance. If a little nation is
trampled upon by a big neighbor who proves
to be a bully and a brute, then another nation
is certainly justified in coming to the out-
raged nation's rescue. And, thus, there seems
to be no escape from the conclusion that on
Christian principles a nation may be not only
justified in going to war, but may be condemned if she refuses to do so. It looks as
though, sometimes, it might be the duty of
a Christian to fight, and that to die on the
battlefield for humanity might be as noble as
to die for truth and justice in a dungeon or
on the scaffold. The advocates of absolute
non-resistance have never established their
case — so it seems to me — either in the court
of common sense, or in the court of Christian teaching. Christ left the question of war

open. It is not a question which can be legislated on in one century, for all the centuries which are to follow. War is indeed brutality, but it must sometimes be met by a counter brutality in order to prevent a wider brutalization of the world. It is in very truth savagery, but the weapons on one side must be met by similar weapons on the other side to hold the world from falling into the permanent grip of a savage. If Charles Martel and his Christian army had not met and overthrown the advancing hosts of Mohammedanism, then all Europe would have passed under the blighting power of the Crescent. If Holland had not resisted the Duke of Alva, then Philip II would have forged chains which might never have been broken. If England had not met and overcome the Spanish Armada, Roman Catholicism would have gotten a new grip on the English people. If England and Germany had not overthrown Napoleon, that monster of ambition would have caused new rivers of blood to flow. If Washington had not resisted the tyranny of Great

Britain, the American Republic could not have entered on her glorious career. And if Abraham Lincoln had not called for volunteers, the Republic would have been torn in twain and the shackles of the slaves would have remained, we know not for how long, unbroken. All wars are evil. They are created by the passions of wicked men. But wicked men may at times so poison and inflame a nation that war against it becomes unescapable. We are to live peaceably with all men as far as it lies within us, but there are times when to live peaceably with some men is impossible, and when the only deliverance from intolerable cruelty or tyranny lies through the blood of the battlefield.

We are living in a world in which there are many undeveloped people, and many perverted people, people who are diseased, or brutalized, or demonized, and gentle methods are consequently not always adequate. When human beings are defective in reason, and deficient in conscience, and have not the full use of the distinctively human faculties, being in fact largely animals or creatures still lower, then coercion seems to be one of the methods which God intends shall be used. At any rate, the use of it is attended by his blessing, and does not violate the conscience of a great majority of the most earnest and faithful Christian men.

I am forced, therefore, to admit the possible occurrence of situations in which the use of force by one nation against another is both rational and beneficial, and therefore Christian. But such situations come but seldom, and as men grow in the Christian spirit, they will come less frequently, and finally they will not come at all.

If it is said that Christ refused to use a sword, and forbade Peter to use a sword, and that therefore nations are forbidden by his precept and example to use a sword, my reply is that Jesus came to found a spiritual kingdom — a kingdom, as he said, "not of this world" — and that Peter was one of his agents in carrying out his plan. In the establishment of a spiritual kingdom no use of force is permissible. As Christian ministers we can never use compulsion in converting men. But we as citizens of the world are under obligation to keep society from falling into chaos while this spiritual kingdom is slowly rising, and there are times when the interests of society are best conserved by the use of force. Had Rome suddenly ceased to use the sword in the first century, Christianity would have been crushed along with every other good thing, in the ruins of the Empire. Paul was always glad to throw himself, when his life was threatened, under the protection of the Roman sword. It was this sword which made it possible, humanly speaking, for him to do his work. We Christians to-day do all our work for Christ under the protection of the state, which owes not a little of its efficiency to its employment of the instruments of coercion. It protects itself day by day from enemies within by the use of force, and it has the same right, no doubt, to protect itself in the same manner from all enemies without. The extreme pacifists are noble men, but they are in my judgment mistaken. I cannot go with them.

Having considered the way in which the New Testament may be misused by the advocates of non-resistance, let us now turn to the devices of those militarists who are always wresting the Scriptures into support of their principles and policies.

In the twenty-fourth chapter of the first gospel, Jesus is reported to have said: "Ye shall hear of wars and rumors of wars: see that ye be not troubled, for all these things must come to pass, but the end is not yet." What shall we infer from this? that wars are a part of the world's plan, a feature of the divine order, beneficent incidents in the unfolding drama? Shall we say that wars are ordained of God, planned in heaven, expedients devised by infinite wisdom for the education and discipline of a race which cannot be trained in any other way? If this be the correct interpretation, then wars should not be looked upon with horror or even regret. We should not strive to head them off,

or to shorten them, but allow them to work
out their foreordained ends. But surely a
better interpretation is possible. When Jesus
said: " These things must come to pass," he
was not thinking of the wise provisions of
God, but of the ignorance and fury of man.
Wars are indeed inevitable, but it is because
of man's folly and wickedness, and not because of the divine planning. All wars are
planned on earth. All wars are the result of
human sin. When Jesus looked out upon the
population of Palestine, seething like a caul-
dron, men's hearts full of vanity and ambition and greed, he knew that out of this condition of heart nothing but devastation and
bloodshed could come. The Jews of the first
century hated Rome with an implacable hatred. Their fingers itched to tear the crown
from Cæsar's head. When passion and
fanaticism rule the heart of a nation, that nation is certain to plunge headlong into war.
Wars are a part of the world plan not by the
good pleasure of God, but by the foolish
choice of man. It is not God's will that men

shall kill one another; they kill one another
because sin has blinded their eyes and they
know not what they do. Our Lord said:
" It must needs be that offenses come, but
woe to him by whom the offense comes."
And so we can say: " It must needs be that
wars come — considering man's stupidity and
brutishness and wickedness — but woe to the
nation by which the war comes." Let us not
forget the last clause in the sentence — " the
end is not yet." War is not the last chapter
in human history. Bloodshed is not the final
word. War occurs in the initial stages.
War is only preliminary, incidental, transi-
tory. The end of the world is harmony. The
last word is peace.

In the twenty-second chapter of the third
gospel it is written: " He that hath no sword,
let him sell his garment and buy one," or in
our vernacular: " Sell your coat and buy a
sword." Strange words indeed to fall from
the lips of the Prince of Peace! The militarist has seized upon them, and uses them
with glee. Let us see what they mean. A

sentence which is obscure, must always be read in the light of other sentences whose meaning is clear.   On the very night on which Jesus said: "Sell your coat and buy a sword," he said to one of his disciples who ventured to use his sword: "Put up your sword; for all who take the sword shall perish by the sword."   The next morning Jesus was arraigned before Pontius Pilate, and Pilate asked him: "Art thou a king?" Jesus replied: "I am," and when he saw how amazed the Roman Procurator was because Jesus had none of the paraphernalia of royalty and carried nothing in his hand, the prisoner went on to say: "If my kingdom were of this world, then would my servants fight.   But now is my kingdom not from hence."   It seems clear then from these two sentences, that Jesus had no intention of using a sword himself or allowing his disciples to use one.   Jesus died upon the cross making no effort to overthrow his foes, and all the apostles, with one exception, met violent deaths, not one of them ever having defended himself with steel. When, therefore, Jesus says: "Sell your coat and buy a sword," he is speaking in vivid and piercing metaphors. He has now reached the end of his career, and he reminds his friends that from this time onward they will meet a set of conditions different from those they faced at the beginning. At first they went out with no provisions, throwing themselves entirely on the hospitality of those to whom they brought their message. In many a home they found a cordial greeting, and all their needs were supplied by the generosity of kind hearted friends. But now the temper of the world has changed. Men realize what the new religion is. They see that it means the condemnation of their favorite sins, and the abandonment of customs in which they take delight. Henceforth, he says, you will meet a hostile world. Homes will be shut against you. Men will suspect and hate you. You will have to fight every step of the way. You will be obliged to take care of yourself. Others will not assist you. You must sell your coat, give up all idea of comfort, and buy a sword, supply yourself with the keen edge of an aggressive spirit. Be prepared to attack the hosts which come out to meet you. You cannot conquer unless you defy the world. The sentence, " Sell your coat and buy a sword," is like this other sentence, " If your right hand offend you, cut it off," and like this, " If your right eye offend you pluck it out," and like this, " If you have faith as a grain of mustard seed, you can say to this mountain, remove, and it will remove." They are all vivid, picturesque, arresting, thought compelling and unforgetable.

Of course the disciples misunderstood him. They were always doing that. Their wits were dull. One day he said to them: " Beware of the leaven of the Pharisees and Sadducees," and they began at once to think of loaves of bread baked in Pharisaic ovens. He was saddened by their stupidity. " Do you not yet understand me?" he said, " Can you not see that I am not thinking of bread? I am thinking of ideas. They are mighty forces in this world. They mould human lives, and fix the fate of empires. False ideas are the deadliest of all forces. The ideas of the leading religious men of your day are false, beware of them." And so when he says, " Sell your coat and buy a sword," the disciples, like little children, bring out two bits of sharpened steel, saying: " Here are two swords!" O the pathos of it! The idea of meeting the panoplied hosts of the mightiest military empire known to history by two little blades of steel! Jesus, looking upon them with pity, says, with a sigh, " It is enough." In other words, " Let us drop the subject. Let us talk of something else." The disciples may be pardoned for their stupidity for they lived in the early dawn, but what excuse can you make for grown men in the twentieth century, who find in the words of Jesus, " Sell your coat and buy a sword," divine warrant for the use of howitzers!

In the tenth chapter of the first gospel Jesus is reported as saying: " Think not that I came to send peace on earth: I came not to send peace but a sword." This is one of the most quoted of all our Lord's sayings, and the militarist makes use of it in season and out of season. Jesus is alleged to be declaring in these words his supreme purpose, and that purpose is nothing less than the stirring up of wars. Jesus desires progress, and wars are essential to progress, and therefore wherever the Christian religion goes, you must expect battlefields red with slaughter. Jesus was no sentimentalist, we are told, he did not shrink from the idea of war. Perpetual peace is only an iridescent dream — and not a beautiful dream at that, as Von Moltke long ago asserted. The idea that nations can live together in peace is a fancy of incorrigible visionaries. The Lord of Life knows what this world is in need of, and so he comes to give a larger place to the sword.

In order to understand these words, we must glance at the context, the words which go before and the words which come after. No sentence of a discourse can be rightly interpreted if isolated, and robbed of the illuminating power which lies in the sentences around it. This particular sentence is a part of a charge which Jesus delivered to twelve young men about to set out on a tour for preaching his gospel of love. He began by reminding them that they were going on a hazardous mission. They were being sent like sheep into the midst of wolves. Sheep hurt nobody. Wolves snap and bite and lacerate and kill. The world is like a wolf, it will not hesitate to destroy. But you, he said, are to be sheep: you are not permitted to hurt anybody. You are to be always harmless. If there is any killing to be done, it must be done by the wolves. After painting a catalogue of the tribulations and sufferings which they might reasonably expect, and after telling them that even if men killed them their fate was not to be deplored, for there are worse things in this world than being killed, he goes on to add: "Think not that I come to send peace on earth, I come not to send peace but a sword." We have here infinitives not of purpose, as the grammarians say, but of result. Do not think that the immediate result of my gospel is going to be tranquillity, calm, repose! There was danger of them thinking just that. After the long centuries of tumult and strife, men's hearts were hungry for peace. And now if Jesus were indeed the promised Messiah, it was natural that men should expect him to usher in at once an age of universal harmony and good will. He warns them against this expectation. "Do not think," he said, "that justice is going to be established without protest, that truth is going to be crowned without opposition, that love is going to be enthroned without strife. Do not dream that the principle of righteousness is going to be set up in the kingdom of life in the midst of tranquillity, and by the universal approbation of consenting minds. The immediate effect of the proclamation of my principles will be fresh controversy, increased dissension, more violent commotion and struggle. In many cases the strife will cut deep into the family circle. A son will be against his father, a daughter against her mother, a daughter-in-law against her mother-in-law. The young people will respond to my high idealism more readily than their parents. But no matter what it costs, one must be faithful to the truth. This is my gospel; go, teach it. You do not labor in vain. So finely is the universe adjusted, that if a man gives in the right spirit, even a cup of cold water, the heavens will open and the blessing of God descend.

Is Jesus in this charge discussing questions of diplomacy or considering the duties and rights of nations? No. Nations are not in all his thoughts. He is talking to twelve ministers, and he warns them not to expect humanity to accept the truth without controversies and conflicts and struggles. The word " sword " is a metaphor. It stands for strife.

There is only one act of our Lord which has been claimed to lend support to the doctrine of militarism, and that is his cleansing

of the temple.   It is easy to read into the story
more than is there.   Jesus has often been
painted by imaginative artists in a towering
rage beating men with a ponderous whip, and
smashing everything which came in his way.
The Evangelists record no such scene.   It
seems from what they say that when he saw
the shameless desecration of the temple he
hastily twisted some cords lying on the floor
into a whip, and by waving this in the air he
started the sheep and steers out of the temple.
It is not certain that he struck one of them.
It is inconceivable to any one really acquainted
with the Jesus of the New Testament that he
struck a man.   He struck the men with nothing but the keen glance of his reproachful
eyes.   When he looked at them and said:
"Take these things hence," they obeyed.
They were not afraid of his whip: they cow-
ered before his soul. Like guilty things
afraid they slunk away. Desperate indeed
must be the cause of a man who in order to
prove that war is justifiable goes to the story
of the cleansing of the temple.

This, then, is certain: the man of men re-
lies upon a power for the conquest of the
world mightier than physical force. The
kingdom of good will is to be built up by
persuasion. The peoples of the world are to
be brought into a gentler temper by the potent persuasiveness of a loving heart. The
exile on Patmos sometimes, in his mind's eye,
saw the King of kings and Lord of lords
seated on a war horse, and riding at the head
of a vast and conquering army. The leader
carried indeed a sword, but he carried it in
his mouth. The weapon with which Christ
conquers is his message. His sword is a
word, and that word is love. It is the sharp-
est and longest and mightiest of all swords.
It is the chosen weapon of the King of kings.

When Paul exhorts us to put on the whole
armor of God, he closes his catalogue of
weapons with the sword. It is the sword of
the Spirit, he says, or, in other phrase, it is
the word of God. Paul always is careful to
make it clear that the weapons of our warfare
are not carnal. We are to conquer by the

spirit of fraternity, good will, forgiveness, compassion, love. How long will mankind be plagued and tormented by war? Until men grow sick of the armor of Cæsar, and consent to put on the armor of God.

III

The Church and Peace

EVERYBODY seems to take it for granted that the Christian church is committed to the principle of peace. The birth of Jesus was announced by angels singing of peace, and for 1900 years the founder of the church has borne the title " Prince of Peace." None of his sayings are better known than: " Blessed are the peacemakers, for they shall be called the sons of God," and " Blessed are the meek, for they shall inherit the earth." His great exhortation: " Love your enemies, and pray for them that persecute you " has made a profound impression on the mind of the world. Everybody knows that the religion of Christ proclaims a message of love, and ascribes an immeasurable value to every human being. Men who know nothing else of

the Christian religion know that it proclaims
the fatherhood of God, and the brotherhood
of man. The man in the street has forgotten
much that he learned when a boy, but he remembers that Christ declared the first and
great commandment to be, "Love God," and
the second, "Love your neighbor as yourself." The outside world is quite perplexed
then over the fact that the Christian church
has never been more zealous in the cause of
peace. The longer one ponders the matter,
the more mysterious it becomes that profess-
ing Christians have never in the mass taken a
bold stand against war. Wherever the Christian religion goes, it carries with it a book, in
the first part of which there is a picture of a
bonfire in which the paraphernalia of war is
being consumed, and in the second part of
which there is a picture of a beautiful city
coming down from God out of heaven.
Christians are expected to pray without ceas-
ing: "Thy kingdom come, Thy will be
done on earth as it is done in heaven"—and
it is difficult to see how the city of God can

come down and rest upon a world covered
with howitzers and lyddite shells. The
foundations of the city which the New Testament promises flash like gems, and it is inconceivable that for gems we are permitted
to substitute instruments of slaughter. It
seems to be absurd for nations to keep praying, Thy kingdom come, when they go on
coining their treasure into swords and guns.
The world a long time ago accepted the test
suggested by Jesus: " By their fruits ye
shall know them," and the present generation
insists on judging the church by what it is
able to do. For many years the question has
been uppermost in the minds of thoughtful
men, is the Christian religion practicable, or
is it only a dazzling dream? Are the principles of Christ workable, or are they only
the brilliant suggestions of a beautiful mind?
Are his commandments binding on diplomats
and rulers, or are they only poetic sentences
to be memorized by Sunday school boys and
girls? Is the Golden Rule for empires as
well as for individuals? Are nations to for-

give, or men only? Has the great commandment binding force upon statesmen or are they privileged to act under a different law? Are patience and compassion and tenderness and forbearance and sacrifice wholesome virtues in the realm of international life? Is it Utopian to expect nations to do justice and love mercy and walk humbly before God?

These questions were often in men's minds during the last two decades of armed peace, and since the opening of the present war the questions have become more importunate and piercing. The questions now uppermost are: What has the church done? What good has it accomplished? What truths has it succeeded in writing on the mind of the world? It has claimed to be a divinely inspired teacher — what has it taught? It has professed to be the representative of God on earth. Has it faithfully represented him? Where is its promised power? Does it not stand impotent in the hour of the world's greatest need? If it was dowered with heavenly authority, why could it not hold Europe back from plunging into this abyss of blood and tears? There are many who pass from questions to affirmations. They declare boldly that the church has been discovered to be incompetent and useless. Others say that the Christian religion has broken down, Christ taught a religion which the world will never accept, and which is not adequate to meet the needs of our modern world. It is declared that the Man of Galilee was not the one who was to come, and that we are now forced to look for another.

What shall we say in reply to all this? Let us first of all say frankly that the Church of Christ has been in large measure recreant to its trust. The church in all lands has failed lamentably to do its full duty. It has everywhere put emphasis on anise and cummin, and neglected the weightier matters of the law. It has squandered too much time on sacrifice, and forgotten that God's chief demand is mercy. It has spent too much of its energies on questions of ritual and sacraments and church government, and not given the great principle of love the place which Christ gave it. The pulpit has in no Christian land been faithful in proclaiming the great fact that God has made of one all the nations of the earth. Nowhere has it taught with fidelity and passion the new commandment: " Love one another as I have loved you." Christ says that love is the badge of Christian discipleship, that it is the proof of genuine discipleship, and that it is the one irrefutable evidence that he came down from heaven. The new commandment has never had a place in the great creeds of the church. When the church goes up into the temple to pray, it must not take the strut of the Pharisee, but the humble attitude of the Publican, crying, " God be merciful to me the sinner."

The principle of union of church and state has worked disastrously in Christian history from the day it was first adopted under Constantine down to the present hour. Wherever it has been tried it has worked havoc with religion. Whenever the ministers of Christ become the salaried officials of the state, they subject themselves to a pressure which is not wholesome. There is forced upon them a conservatism which is hostile to progress, and they are in danger of being brought into subjection to ideals which are contrary to the ideals of Christ. Strong men, in isolated instances, have been able to withstand these influences, but the mass of the clergy have always been prone to defer too much to the ruling sentiment and policy of the state. A false distinction has been made between the secular and the sacred, and the minister of Christ has contented himself with preparing souls for the next world while the ministers of state have gone on unhindered to rule men after their own will in this world. The clergy of the Russian church have done many noble and beautiful things, but who would dare say that the Russian church has been faithful to the cause of humanity during the last thousand years? Has not that church put too much emphasis on the importance of kissing icons or sacred pictures, and on the value of a pilgrimage to the Jordan river, while large areas of life have been totally neglected, civil officials being allowed to mould and direct the life of the people? Roman Catholicism has performed many a noble service to humanity. Her contribution to civilization is varied and invaluable. Many of her priests have been men of great courage, and magnificent character, but is it to be denied that in every Roman Catholic country too much stress has been placed on Paternosters and Ave Marias, and too much power has been ascribed to the saints in the next world, and too much thought has been given to purgatory and hell, and not sufficient attention has been bestowed upon that kingdom of love which is to be established in the hearts and homes of men? The Lutheran church of Germany has an illustrious record. To the end of time the world will be indebted to her scholars and saints, but who would dare say that the Lutheran clergy have for the last forty years been faithful in proclaiming the central truths of the Christian religion? Much has been said about justification by faith, and the doctrine of consubstantiation. Children have been instructed in the catechism and have been trained to repeat the commandments and the Lord's Prayer, but what has the Lutheran church done on the whole to check the growth of militarism and to build up in the German people a Christian attitude to Slavs and Frenchmen? It has been in Germany as it has been in the Greek and Roman Catholic countries. The ministers of religion, salaried by the state, have not been free to discuss national policies, or to criticise and condemn the action of the ministers of state, the result being that Europe has been ruled for the most part by men who have slight knowledge of Christian principles, and even slighter inclination to put these principles into practice. When you close the mouths of the ministers of Christ on national policy you give free scope to the Machiavellis and the Metternichs and the Clausewitzes and the Sharnhorsts and the Bernhardis, and then certain good people are surprised that civilization should get into a ditch! This world cannot

get on without the faithful application of
Christian principles to national affairs.
There is none other name under heaven
whereby we must be saved, but the name of
Jesus. Statesmen who reject his principles
are only leading nations to their doom.
Christ is a stone which diplomats and rulers
can reject, but they reject him to their everlasting loss. It is forever true: " He that
falleth on this stone shall be broken to pieces;
but on whomsoever it shall fall, it will scatter
him as dust."

The Anglican church has also been recreant
to its duty. Individual leaders have spoken
and written brave and telling words, but the
Anglican church has never put forth its
mighty strength to make war upon war.
English churchmen have in appalling numbers
apologized for every war in which Great
Britain has ever had a part. Even the Boer
war was defended by them. War has not
seemed hideous to the average Englishman
because the Anglican church has been silent
when it should have spoken in tones of thun-

der. The non-conformist pulpit of Great
Britain has been far in advance of the Anglican in endeavoring to create a conscience
against national aggression and snobbery, and
to build up a more Christian temper in dealing with the nations of the earth.

In our own country our churches have also
been remiss. Our ministers have not been
gagged by entanglements with the state, but
we have been dominated by an individualist
gospel, and preachers with few exceptions
have let what they call politics alone. They
have been satisfied to save souls and let the
nation get on as it could. Men who are
averse to taking an interest in civic conditions, are still less inclined to devote themselves to international affairs, and so the
clergy of the United States have, on the whole,
allowed the international problem to lie outside their province. It has been left for a
handful of naval experts and the Navy
League, and a few congressional hotheads,
and a small company of Jingo editors to determine what our naval policy shall be. We

have within a few years spent over two billion dollars on our navy, and this navy is to-day, according to naval experts, absolutely inadequate to protect us from any foe who cares to land upon our shore. Although there are thirty-three millions of confessed Christians in our country, it is doubtful if we should have squandered more money on battleships than we have, if we had all been infidels or Mohammedans or Apache Indians. The Church of Christ exerts, directly, only a feeble and fluctuating influence on the spirit and policy of our government.

For many years the impotency of organized Christianity in the realm of world politics has been an open scandal. The church has long since ceased to be considered a national factor among the forces working for peace. During the last twenty years when men have looked around for a possible escape from the crushing burdens of militarism, and for a bulwark against war, they have turned to the bankers, or to the merchants, or to the scientists, or to the Socialists, or to the humanitarians, rather than to church members for deliverance. It has been claimed that the bankers of the world would not permit great nations to rush into war, and that the leaders of commerce would never suffer the business of the world to be thrown into chaos, and that science would render the instruments of destruction so deadly that men would refuse to fight any more, and that the Socialists with their doctrine of comradeship and their policy of international coöperation would block any effort of parliaments and rulers to induce wage earners to fight one another, and that humanitarians, lovers of their kind, would rise up in horror at the very beginning of war and compel the carnage to stop, but seldom has any one suggested that the Christian church might have anything to do in preventing a world baptism of blood. The church is the greatest of all organizations, possessing more men and more money than any other, its fundamental doctrine is love, and it carries at the front the banner of the cross, proclaiming its belief in sacrificial service, and yet in the twentieth century when men look for a savior from the burden of armaments and for a refuge from the war-tempest, they look in every other direction rather than toward the Christian church!

This must be because of the record which the church has made. The church has at times engaged in war herself. She has been the leader in wars, and when she has not herself led, she has consecrated the flags which the nations have carried into battle. She has sanctioned wars in her councils, and invoked on them the blessing of heaven. She has had all sorts of excuses and apologies and defenses for every war that has ever been waged. The Russian church did not throw itself against the war of Russia with Japan, nor did the Anglican church throw itself against the war of Great Britain with the Boers, nor did American organized Christianity hurl itself against our war with Spain. These were among the most inexcusable and indefensible wars of the last quarter of a century, and yet the majority of the leaders of the Church of Christ either openly approved them, or maintained a consenting silence.

It is this failure of the church to take a bold and firm stand on the great moral issues of mankind, to hurl itself with crushing force upon the acknowledged evils of history that give the ungodly a chance to blaspheme. Men say in derision: "What do Christians more than others? They are precisely like other men. After all their Bible reading and sermon listening, and praying, they are no more enthusiastic for righteousness and no more hostile to evil than are many men who never pray at all and who make no Christian professions." It is not uncommon to find outside the church, among the unbelievers and agnostics, men of clearer insight and nobler moral passions than can be found in many church officials.

If the attitude of the church toward armed peace was such as to provoke contempt among large numbers of forward looking men, this contempt broke into open derision when, last August, the great war began. At once a

fierce cry of condemnation of the church went
up around the world. All the enemies of the
church lifted up their voices together. The
skeptic uttered his gibe and the infidel got in
his jeer. All the questioning and doubting
souls were pushed down into a deeper doubt.
They had surmised that Christ, possibly, was
the one who was to redeem the world, but the
collapse of Christian civilization filled their
hearts with misgivings. All the lukewarm
friends of the church stood off at a greater
distance, and all believers whose faith had
been weak, felt the foundations quivering beneath them. Men who had been on the edge
of unbelief were pushed over, and men in
whose minds the ferment of doubt had been
at work, suddenly reached final conclusions,
and their decision was rendered against the
church. There was no end to the sarcastic
questions: " Is this Christianity? Is this the
outcome of Christian teaching? Is this the
best that the Church of Christ can do? " It
was a rare opportunity for the cartoonist, and
he at once began to give us pictures of Chris-

tian nations flying at one another's throats, while astonished barbarians and savages looked on in amazement, wondering if the interests of humanity did not demand that they should interfere. In magazines and papers men of literary force and fame began to discuss the failure of the church, and some of them exploited in vivid phrases the failure of Christianity. An English novelist expressed the feeling of many hearts when he wrote in an American magazine: "Three hundred thousand church spires raised to the glory of Christ. Three hundred million human beings baptized into his service! And — war to the death of them all! Let your hearts beat to God and your fists in the face of the enemy. God on the lips of each potentate, and under three hundred thousand spires prayer that twenty-two million servants of Christ may receive from God the blessed strength to tear and blow each other to pieces, to ravage and burn, to wrench husbands from wives, fathers from their children, to starve the poor, and everywhere destroy the works of the spirit.

Prayer under three hundred thousand spires for the blessed strength of God to use the noblest, most loyal instincts of the human race to the ends of carnage! God be with us to the death and dishonor of our foes! The God who gave his only begotten Son to bring on earth peace and good will toward men. No creed — in these days when two and two are put together — can stand against such reeling subversion of the foundation. After this monstrous mocking, beneath this grinning skull of irony, how shall there remain faith in a religion preached and practiced to such ends?"

Such feelings in time of great excitement are natural and indeed inevitable, but one must be careful, when under the strain of powerful feeling, not to allow himself to be swept into foolish and unjust judgments. Wholesale condemnations are always wrong. Extreme declarations have to be retracted. The church is by no means perfect, but we must deal with her fairly. She has not done everything, but we must give her credit for

what she has done. She is without doubt a
sinner, but we must, if truly Christian, be the
friend of publicans and sinners. We are not
to condone her sin, or to try to cover up her
sin, but we are not to gloat over her sin, and
by our refusal to give sympathy or assistance
push her down into still deeper sin. The
church, like the home and the state, has never
done all that she could, and for the same
reason. All three institutions are heavily
weighted with human nature. All three are
made out of the dust of the earth, and when
institutions are built out of imperfect human
beings you cannot expect that their conduct
shall be ideal. They will fall short at a hundred points, but since God is patient with them
we must be patient too. We do not make
things better by trampling on the home, or
by abolishing the state. With all their defects
and blunderings, we cannot get on without
them. Neither can we get on without the
church. The important question is: How
can we improve it? The first step is to get
into cordial and sympathetic relations with it,

to look at it out of friendly eyes, to take note
of the invaluable service which it has rendered
to mankind. From the beginning, it has
waged war against war, even though it has
not always been conscious of what it has done,
and even though in speech it has at times
seemed to preach the gospel of Cæsar. The
church is always hostile to war, no matter
what the preachers say, for the reason that
the church reads to the people the Gospels,
and teaches men to repeat the Lord's Prayer.
It is impossible to train human beings to pray
the Lord's Prayer without working against
every form of social evil. The church worked
against slavery even when Christian preachers
defended it. It is impossible to preach the
parables of Jesus and unfold his cardinal doc-
trines without hastening the day when slavery
shall be no more. Christian preachers often
build better than they know. They accomplish ends at which they do not aim. They
bring the world blessings for which they do
not ask. The ministers of Christ have often
seen but dimly the implications of the gospel

they proclaimed, but the Holy Spirit taking the words of Jesus, interprets them to the world's heart, and thus in spite of clerical ignorance and stupidity and cowardice, the word of the Lord runs and is glorified. It is not true that in spite of all that has been said in the course of the centuries, war has been continued as if not a word had been spoken. There is not so much fighting now as there was before Jesus came. There is not so much as there was a thousand years ago, or five hundred years ago. It was once difficult for the church to secure a truce even for two or three days in a week, and now whole years and decades elapse in which great nations do not unsheathe the sword. History tells us that there have been seven years' wars, and thirty years' wars, and even a hundred years' war, but to us, the thought of a war so long drawn out is intolerable. Even a war six months long seems to us interminable, and no sooner has it begun than we begin to ask how many weeks it is going to continue. War is abnormal to us, upsetting, depressing, monstrous, why? Because we have breathed the atmosphere of the Christian church. The church has not yet made wars impossible, because she has not yet gotten hold of the hearts of potentates and diplomats, but she is slowly creating a mood and a temper in the hearts of the masses of the people which will some day render it impossible for the craziest of emperors and the stupidest of statesmen to plunge nations into mutual slaughter. When men ask what has the church done, let us reply that it has so sensitized the heart that it cries out in horror at spectacles which centuries ago excited no comment. There are now millions of human beings who cannot think of war except with a shudder, and every new tale of butchery only deepens in them a spirit of indignation and protest which will some day burn up the ancient abomination. It is this growing spirit of implacable opposition to war makers and their trade which renders the abolition of war absolutely certain. The time is coming when men will not endure it. It is the shudder of the Christian heart which will by and by shatter the apparatus of war to pieces.

What wonderful advances the world has made, and the Christian church has helped to make them. How little we hear nowadays about military glory. The chivalry and shimmer of warfare have well-nigh disappeared. No one seems to exult in the glorious privilege of killing men. The foolish talk which continued through many centuries, of war being a school for the virtues, has been laughed out of all circles which are not hopelessly benighted. To the modern eye war is horrible, hideous, damnable, and the reason it is this, is because the church has taught the world to look at things through the eyes of Jesus. In the olden times kings offered no excuses when they went to war. It was not necessary for them to justify themselves at any tribunal. No one asked if their cause was right. The only concern was about their strength. And now, behold, a whole continent of rulers, all holding up their hands, protesting that they are not responsible for this war. In all the circle of the kings there is not one who dares stand forth and say: " I caused this war. I wanted it, and I worked to make it inevitable." Every man of them declares that he is altogether innocent, that he did his utmost to preserve the peace, and that the sword has been forced into his hands. And what the rulers say, the statesmen are all repeating. Not one of them is willing to confess that he had anything to do with causing this frightful conflagration. Every nation is fighting solely in self-defense. Servia is fighting for her life, and so is Austria, and so are Russia, Germany, France and Great Britain. We have been told this a dozen times by leaders in all these countries. Every diplomat in Europe has his hands in a basin of water, declaring, after the fashion of Pontius Pilate, that any blood shed must rest on the heads of other men. This is an extraordinary phenomenon in human history. Nothing like it has ever been seen before. How can we explain it? There is no explanation except that the Christian church by its pictures of Jesus and the Madonna, and its hymns of love, and its prayers for the Holy

Spirit, has so changed the natural temper of
the heart that what men once delighted in they
now abhor. How careful statesmen now are
in drawing distinctions between wars of aggression and wars of defense. They all condemn the former and defend the latter only.
Christian nations are no longer willing to appropriate money for guns to be used in attacking other nations. The only way to get the
money is to avow that every cent of it shall
be spent for defense. How strange such talk
would have seemed to Alexander the Great,
and to Julius Cæsar. How unintelligible to
Attila and Tamerlane. How silly to Frederick the Great, and how preposterous to the
great Napoleon. Why this carefulness to discriminate between different kinds of wars?
Why this scrupulosity about entering upon
wars of aggression? There is no other explanation than this: The church has created
a conscience, a living soul under the ribs of
death.

And note still further what the church has
done. It has created a heart which cannot en-

dure sufferings which were unalleviated in the wars of the non-Christian world. The Red Cross is one of the creations of the religion of Jesus. Such an organization was unknown in the pre-Christian world. The church has not been able to put an end to war, but it has created in the hearts of men and women a mighty pity, so that when through folly and wickedness war is precipitated, a host of physicians and nurses spring to their feet, eager to care for the wounded and to comfort the dying. In the very hell of war this flower of paradise has blossomed. It is an evidence of the power of Christ to keep alive the sentiment of pity. The church cannot yet restrain the madness of stupid statesmen, but it will reduce somewhat the pain, and lighten a little the horror which war inevitably brings. It will send an angel of mercy to assuage the agony of an experience which it is not yet able to prevent. It has not done everything, but it has done something. It has failed, but its failure is not total.

And, moreover, its work is not yet completed. The church is not old yet, as God measures time. It is only a child, just beginning to learn how to live and labor. It has had many things to do in the last two millenniums, more things than could be completed in so short a period. Spiritual processes are slow. You cannot secure harvests to-morrow or next week. You must wait. Sometimes you must wait for years, sometimes for a generation, sometimes for centuries, sometimes for a thousand years. The greater the work the more time needed for the accomplishment. The more glorious the harvest, the longer you must wait after the planting of the seed. The church has been taunted from the beginning by impatient critics who have demanded that every needed thing should be done forthwith. Never has the world been more impatient than it is now. The inventions of science and the rapidity of material progress have begotten in our generation a fever of haste which renders us incapable of trusting ourselves with calm hearts to the slow and long-drawn processes of spiritual evolution. Whatever we want we want now. If war ought to cease, then why not stop it to-day? If the church is going to establish peace, why not do it at once? The answer is easy. The church cannot do things at once. Jesus of Nazareth died with all his greatest projects unfinished. When he closed his eyes on the cross, Jerusalem was unconverted, Palistine was practically untouched by his gospel, and the great outside world was in total ignorance of what he had said and done. Civic government in Jerusalem was as sordid as it was when he found it, slavery was as firmly established in human society on the day of his death as on the day of his birth, the Roman empire was as rotten after his prayers and his teachings as it was before he left the little carpenter shop in Nazareth. But he was not at all daunted. Lack of immediate success did not discourage him. The failure of the world to respond did not quench the hope in his heart. He was willing to wait on the Lord. He had confidence in the vitality of the seed he had planted. He believed in God and in himself and in man. Even with all the world turning against him he dared say: "And I, if I be lifted up will draw all men unto me." Love cannot conquer in a minute, but love, he was certain, will conquer in the end. And so in spite of opposition and rebuff and failure, he moved toward the cross with the stride of a conqueror, saying to his friends: "Be of good cheer, I have overcome the world."

It is in this spirit that we must approach the Christian church. We are to reverence her for what she is going to do. For centuries she has planted seed, and this seed was not sown in vain. It will some day bring forth rich harvests to God's glory. There have been many storms, and numberless inclement seasons, and the delays have been long and discouraging, but the end is certain. The church was founded upon a rock and the gates of Hades shall not prevail against it. War is one of her enemies, and over war as over slavery, and many another savage custom, she will ultimately come off more than conqueror.

When men rail against the Christian church, they should remember that she is not the only culprit in the world. Why not rail at science? For three generations she has been the world's most conspicuous miracle worker. Like a wizard she has bewitched the human imagination. She has filled the world with the fame of her mighty deeds. Young men have gone wild over her splendid exploits, and older men have written eulogies, proclaiming that science will be the future religion of the world. She and she alone has the words of eternal life, and to her all coming generations belong. Such has been the hallelujah chorus sounding in our ears. Why not, then, rail at science for not preventing this war? Europe is rich in universities, and the universities are rich in scientists, and the scientists are rich in knowledge, and why did not the scientists of Europe apply their knowledge to the solution of the difficult problem which Europe laid before them? If science is indeed the strongest limbed of all the servants of the Almighty, why in Europe's hour of peril did she not put out her arm, and save the world from this unspeakable calamity? Alas, science was impotent, fully as impotent as the church, and if religion is to be cudgeled for being weak why not cudgel science also? Is not science capable of engaging in an enterprise truly great? Cannot science perform a herculean labor? Is science to be excused from all the world's hardest problems? Is the church alone to be counted responsible for rescue when the fiercest tempests fall?

When it is said that the church has more than once braced men's hearts for battle by her songs and prayers, it can be said in reply that science has ever forged the weapons with which the butchery of war has been carried on. War to-day is more terrible than it has ever been before, because of the assistance which science has rendered. It is she who has created the aëroplane and the explosive bombs, the howitzer and the machine guns, the submarines and the treacherous torpedoes. Without the aid of science, war would be a feeble and comparatively harmless thing. Science has given war a new dimension. It once had but length and breadth, and science has added depth and height. For the first time in history, men are fighting above the clouds and beneath the sea. A new ferocity has been added to the art of war by science. Why not rail at science, and trample on her because she has rushed to the assistance of men starting off to battle!

But where shall we stop if we once begin to apportion the blame for the continuance of war? If the present war is a disgrace to religion, it is also a disgrace to education. Europe has had for centuries great educational establishments. Her faculties contain many of the wisest men in the world. Her philosophers are so famous that men of all nations travel to Europe to sit at their feet. They have mastered the knowledge and wisdom of the centuries. They know the best that has been thought and said. They have studied the principles of life, and have weighed the lessons of human experience. Knowing so much of the past, they certainly ought to know something of the present, and at least a little of the future. For generations wise men have been instructing the young men of Europe. All the leading statesmen and diplomatists of the great powers have been taught by men of vast learning and genius. And yet education has failed. Of what value is education if it does not fit us to live? Why should we covet it, if it does not tell us what to seek and what to avoid? If education cannot save a continent from plunging into hell, why should we tolerate education any longer? Universities and colleges are useless institutions, professors are mischievous pedants and idlers, all education is without value, because in the year of our Lord 1914 ten nations plunged into war! Why not condemn and despise education?

And statesmanship is also disgraced. The Chancelleries of Europe have had what everybody supposed were the shrewdest, and longest headed, and most brilliant men in Europe. They were all experts in the art of diplomacy. It was their business to know not only their own country, but also all the other countries with which their nation had to deal. And yet these diplomatic highbrows were so stupid they could not keep Europe from entering into a frenzy in which they are burning up a large part of her treasure. If you should take out of the lunatic asylums of Europe a hundred of the most brainless of the imbeciles found there, and place the governments of Europe in their hands, they could not get the world into a more deplorable mess than that in which it now writhes. Why put all the blame on the preachers and priests? Why not rail at the statesmen, the diplomats, the cabinet ministers, the mighty men who sit in the seats of power?

If you persist in talking about the disgrace of the church, then talk about the disgrace of reason. If faith has been disgraced, then reason is also disgraced. There never has been a war more stupid and inexcusable than the one which is now raging, and there was not reason enough in Europe to avoid it, and there is not reason enough now to stop it. Reason stands before the world's judgment seat branded with shame. How can we say after this war that man is a rational creature? Where is there convincing evidence of his rationality? Is he not a fit candidate for the insane asylum? Why not confess that common sense is disgraced? We were supposed to have great stores of it, where will you look for it now? When all institutions are disgraced, and when all the human faculties have been weighed in the balance and found wanting, it is singular that so many persons should single out the church as the only culpable institution, and religion as the only culprit deserving castigation! The whole world stands condemned.

But while we may freely confess that organized Christianity has not met its responsibilities, and deserves stern reprimand and censure, we must be careful how far we allow ourselves or others to go in passing condemnation on the Christian religion. The religion of Jesus must be distinguished from the organization which acts as its custodian. The

Christian religion is a heavenly treasure, but
it is carried in an earthen vessel, and when
the vessel develops flaws it does not follow
that the treasure itself is faulty. The body
may be flecked and stained, while the indwell-
ing spirit remains untarnished. The witnesses of Christ may prove unworthy, while
the Master himself remains faultless. The
institution which bears his name may fail,
while he himself continues to conquer. We
must never identify Christianity with so-called
Christian civilization. Because Christian nations go astray it does not follow that Christ
himself has failed us. There are no Christian nations. There is no Christian civilization. We use such terms for convenience, in
distinguishing between different parts of the
world. We call one civilization Confucian,
and another Mohammedan, and another Christian, after the name of the religious teacher
who has made the deepest impress upon that
civilization. But no civilization has ever
been Christian in the sense that it has been
dominated by the spirit of Christ. Christian

civilization, therefore, may fail while the religion of Jesus remains undiscredited. The so-called Christian nations are not built on Christian principles, nor are their policies worked out with an eye single to the commands of Christ. A large part of the population in every so-called Christian nation is not deeply influenced by the Christian spirit, and in no part of a nation's life is the spirit of Christ so little manifested as in the realm of statesmanship. The rulers and legislators, even when baptized into the name of Jesus, have in most cases declared on entering the work of diplomacy, " We shall not have this man to rule over us." Christian nations, therefore, may crumble and fall, while the Christian truth remains unshaken. Christian nations can act on Pagan principles and when they do, their alleged Christianity does not save them. He that sits in the heavens laughs. He breaks them in pieces like a potter's vessel, just as he shattered Nineveh and Babylon and Rome. Even though all the so-called Christian nations should, like the Gadarene swine, rush down a steep place and plunge headlong to destruction, there would be no proof of any defect in the religion of Jesus, or any discrediting of the declaration that he has power to save to the uttermost all who put their trust in him. By Christianity is meant the spirit and teachings of Jesus, and who dare say that these have failed? When has the doctrine of the fatherhood of God been proved absurd, and when has the doctrine of the brotherhood of man proved pernicious? What howitzer has shattered the great commandment? What shell has torn to shreds the Golden Rule? The Golden Rule is golden still, and the breath of the hot cannon's mouth will never tarnish it. The new commandment never looked so lustrous and divine as it looks when viewed through the rifts of the smoke of battle. The principles of kindness and brotherliness and forgiveness and service are principles which the thunder of guns has not shaken. The war has only illustrated our imperious need of them, and their everlasting authority. Not a jot or a tittle of the Christian revelation has passed away since the great war opened. Not one truth announced by Jesus has been undermined. Never before has the founder of Christianity stood forth more manifestly and indisputably the one fairest among ten thousand, the one altogether lovely. He is the unique and incomparable and indispensable Christ. We now realize as never before that he has the words of eternal life, and that nations must submit to him or be broken in pieces. The war is teaching nothing more emphatically than this: that men cannot be Christians in their private life and Pagans in their public policies. There is but one morality for nations and for individuals, and that is the morality of Jesus. He is the Saviour of the individual soul, and he is also the King of kings and Lord of lords. He sits on the throne, and diplomats and rulers must submit to him.

Christianity can never be said to fail until its fundamental teachings are proved to be untrue, or until its essential principles are demonstrated to be unworkable. If what

Christ says is ever proved to be false or impracticable, then we shall admit that Christianity has failed. But the war has not shown the falsity of one of his sentences, nor has it proved that his principles will not work. All that has been shown by the war is that men are still stubborn and hard hearted, and refuse to surrender to God's will. The husbandmen are still wicked, and the heir of the vineyard is still stoned. In that sense and in that only can it be said that Christianity has failed. It has not succeeded in wooing the hearts of the world's rulers. But this is not the fault of Christ, it is the sin of man. God rules the world on the principle of love. Love uses no compulsion. Love will not break down the freedom of the will. Christ says through all the ages: " Behold, I stand at the door and knock: if any man will hear my voice and open the door, I will come in." Christ stands still outside the world's heart. Christianity is the religion of persuasion. It appeals, exhorts, pleads. It leads. It will not drive. The church when true to the spirit of the Master never coerces. It uses none of the instruments of compulsion. It beseeches, and then it waits and hopes and keeps on loving. When at times driven by the fury of impatience, it has attempted to quicken the pace of the world, it has lost time, and retarded human progress. All that the pulpit can do is to say, " Repent ! Seek ye first the Kingdom of God. Love your heavenly Father with all your heart and soul and mind and strength. Love your neighbor as yourself. Look upon all men as your brothers. Let the mind be in you which was also in Christ Jesus. I beseech you in Christ's name be reconciled to God."

This is what the church is already saying. It is going to say it with increased urgency and passion. It is going to place increasing emphasis on the social ideal. It is going to claim boldly all the kingdoms of the world for Christ. It will insist now as it has never insisted before on the application of Christian principles to international affairs. It has had a revelation of the horribleness of war which will never be forgotten. Now that the sword has been whetted to such a murderous edge, Christians will hear more distinctly Christ's great words: " Put up thy sword."

War is going to be hated as it has never been hated before. We know better now what it is. The pictures of the fall of Antwerp with its streaming hosts of refugees, men, women, and little children, the aged, the crippled and the sick, the rich, the poor, the high, the low, all huddled together in one vast mass of helplessness and misery, pouring out of the city under a sky lit up by bursting shells, as though the world had become a blazing and heartbreaking inferno, that picture has been etched into the retina of the world's eye, and it will never fade out. Thousands have been driven finally to the original Quaker position —" War everywhere and always is absolutely unjustifiable and criminal." Millions of others have been confirmed in their conviction that war is never again to be resorted to except as the very last and most desperate resort. As soon as war is made the last resort, in public opinion and state policy, it will never be reached at all. The church is now going to lead in a war against war. Men are everywhere saying: " This must be the last war." Men can make it the last if they will. The church could have ended war long ago. It did not do it. Let us hope that she will now put her hand to the plow, and never again look back. This is the opportunity which God gives the church to prove that she possesses a mission from heaven. There have been three historic scourges: Famine, Pestilence and War. The first two have been slain by science. The last one, science cannot kill. War can be abolished only by love. Science has no control of the heart. To create and nourish the spirit of love is the church's distinctive mission. Other demons have been cast out by lower means, but war, the chief of the world's devils, can be exorcised only by love. In the name of Christ, the church is going to set the world free.

In this work the church has the assistance of numerous agencies and forces which God has created to hasten the accomplishment of

the great task. Many hearts are appalled by
the strength and the number of forces arrayed
against us. When they see the racial antag-
onisms, and the national hatreds, and the commercial rivalries, and the mighty hierarchy of
army and naval officials proud of their titles
and eager to enhance the glory of the great
establishment they serve, and the vast company of war traders, whose profits depend on
swollen budgets for the paraphernalia of war,
and the vociferous and unscrupulous host of
jingo editors and statesmen, and the great
crowd of narrow minded and selfish hearted
citizens whose patriotism is perverted and
whose ideals of life are barbaric, their heart
faints within them, and they cry out in dis-
couragement — Who is sufficient for these
things? But the forces which are with us are
mightier than those which are against us.
We have first of all hundreds of thousands of
Christian ministers, well educated and set
apart as leaders of their congregations. These
men have access to the minds and hearts of
millions of boys and girls who can by them be

trained to abhor war. They have, in their possession, the ideals of the perfect man, and the matchless words of one who spake as never man spake, and every word is a form of power. They have an opportunity given to no other class of men to mould the spirit of the coming generation, and they are going to do it. But other organizations are on our side, and other men, not Christians, are with us. The Jews are with us. Philanthropists of all kinds are with us, and so are the artists, and the scholars, and so are the mighty forces of education and commerce and finance and industry. The wage earners of the world are with us. Fatherhood and motherhood are with us. Womanhood is with us. All the noblest instincts of the human heart cry out trumpet-tongued against the settlement of international disputes by human slaughter. All the best men are with us, in every land, and all the best women, and all the little children. With such cohorts on our side, how is it possible to suffer defeat? All that is needed is that the church shall lead. And the best of

all is that God is with us. His Spirit is on
our side. The universe is fighting against the
men who believe in and produce war. The
stars in their courses fight for us. If the God
of the New Testament is the God who rules
this world, then every sword shall some day
be sheathed, and nations shall make war no
more. The kingdom of God is righteousness
and peace and joy. The city of God is the
city of love and light. War has no place in
a society which has yielded itself to a God of
love. The church is the body of Christ. It
is the instrument by which he is to subdue
all things unto himself. Every minister is by
his ordination a preacher of good will. " How
beautiful on the mountains are the feet of
him that bringeth good tidings, that publisheth
peace."

IV

Christianity and Militarism

IT is not war which Christianity in the twentieth century is called to expose and attack. The enemies of war are legion. Even military chieftains have said damaging things about it. It was the great Napoleon who declared that war is the trade of barbarians, and if our own General Sherman did not assert that war is hell, he called it something else little less complimentary. That war is horrible and brutal and savage, all the world knows, and nearly everybody is ready to acknowledge it. In a sense, all men may be said to be in favor of peace. There is no considerable body of confessed eulogists of war in any section of the civilized world. Even the men who urge huge armies and navies insist they are loyal friends of peace.

The enemy to be faced and conquered in our time is not war, but militarism. Militarism is not war, but it is something out of which war comes. Nobody espouses destruction, but many go in at the wide gate. Militarism is the wide gate. Men are to be classified not by their declared attitude to war, but by their attitude to militarism. We are all agreed as to the beauty of peace and the horror of war. It is only on militarism that men differ.

What is militarism? The word is comparatively new in our American vocabulary. It is necessary to define it. There is much confusion in many minds as to its meaning, and it is used in different senses by different persons. By militarism one man means any display of military equipment whatsoever. A gun is a militarist invention. A keg of powder is another. The marching of a company of the state militia through the street is an exhibition of militarism.

A second man means by militarism, conscript armies and swollen navies. It is not until you get enormous numbers of guns and a desire to display them, that you know what may properly be called militarism. This man would not admit that there is any militarism in the United States. To find it you must go to Europe.

A third man thinks of militarism as an undue exaltation of the military caste. The essence of it lies not in mighty armies or colossal navies, but in the subordination of the civil to the military power. Thus the average Englishman would not admit that there is any militarism in England, because in the first place, the English army is in time of peace comparatively small, and in the second place it has no controlling influence over the policies of the government. When the Englishman wants to see militarism he goes to Prussia, and in the prestige and power of the military class of that part of the German Empire, he finds the genuine article. Militarism is, according to an Englishman, made in Germany. Many Americans have adopted this English notion. We hear much nowadays of German militarism, as though outside of Germany no such thing was in existence. Occasionally a speaker or writer ventures to refer to French or Russian militarism, but the average American does not feel that so long as we have our present diminutive army, and a navy that ranks only third in the list of the world's navies, that the United States can be justly charged with being afflicted by the militarist distemper. Militarism is denounced by all classes of our people. It may be doubted if there is in the United States a man of reputation who would publicly confess himself to be a militarist.

If by militarism we mean belligerency, we certainly are not a militaristic people. We do not hunger and thirst after war. We do not easily quarrel with our neighbors. Our temper is quite pacific. But the same can be said of all the peoples in Europe. No one of them has a belligerent disposition. They are all amiable, quiet, peace-loving peoples. Militarism, then, is something other than belligerency. Nor is militarism simply the maintenance of a military establishment. If we are to measure the dimensions of militarism in a nation by the amount of money expended annually, on army and navy, then the United States is pronouncedly militaristic. We are, if judged thus, a more militaristic nation in one respect than Germany, for within the last sixteen years we have spent over four hundred million dollars more upon our navy than Germany has spent upon hers within the same time. An ingenious German by figuring out the per capita cost of army and navy in the various countries of Europe, has demonstrated that Germany is less militaristic than any of her more powerful neighbors. What do we mean, then, by militarism? When does a nation become militaristic? Who is a militarist?

When we go to the dictionary for light, we read that militarism is " the political condition characterized by the predominance of the military class in government or administration; the tendency to regard military efficiency as the paramount interest of the state." There can be no question that according to this definition, militarism existed in more than one

era of the Roman empire, and that it existed
in France under Napoleon I, and since military preparedness has long been the preferred
business of the Prussian state, and since the
military class holds the place of highest honor
there, we can properly say that militarism exists in Germany. But does militarism exist
nowhere else? Let us consult the dictionary
again. It says that " militarism is the disposition to provide for the strength and safety
of a nation by maintaining strong military
forces." Great Britain then must be counted
among the militarist nations, for she has for
generations counted a mighty fleet essential
to her national welfare. She has claimed and
exercised the right of maintaining a navy
equal to the two next largest navies in the
world, with a certain per cent added to place
her security beyond the reach of doubt. She
has assumed that the great nations of Europe
are her foes, and that they would cripple her
if they could. By means of her navy she has
extended not only her territory but her power,
and some of her greatest writers have declared

that her fighting ships are not only the foundation of her wealth and influence, but the basis also of her very life. According to this definition Great Britain is a militant nation and ours is not. But the dictionary gives us a still wider definition. It says, "Militarism is the spirit and temper which exalts the military virtues and ideals, and minimizes the defects of military training, and the cost of war and preparation for it." If this is militarism, then we have it in the United States. There are thousands of Americans who exalt the military ideals, who do not discern the defects of military training, and who minimize the cost of making preparations for war.

Militarism, then, in the widest sense, is not peculiar to any one nation. It exists in greater or less measure in them all. Germany has had in recent years the largest number of militaristic writers, but that distinction once belonged to France, and all through the history of Great Britain she has had poets and prose writers who have extolled the military virtues, and joined in the apotheosis of war.

What English writers of the nineteenth century would you place above Ruskin and Carlyle? It was Ruskin who said: " All the pure and noble arts of peace are founded on war. There is no great art possible to a nation, but that which is based on battle." And did not Carlyle spend the ripest years of his life in writing a eulogistic history of a military robber and conscienceless liar known as Frederick the Great? An influential section of the English people has always paid obeisance to the god of war.

Militarism is a disease with which all nations are more or less afflicted. Individuals in large numbers in every country are infected by this poison. In some countries, the infected classes are larger than others; in a few countries the virus flows full and strong in the policy of the state.

Militarists then must be classified. They are not all of the same school. The full grown militarist is a man who believes that war is inevitable, that it will never be outgrown, and besides being inevitable, it must be counted a blessing. It is one of the things which the Almighty has provided for man's good. Without it humanity would become stagnant, and the moral fiber of nations would rot. Since war is inevitable and a means of human development, then a nation's first business is to prepare for it. The preparation must be conscientious and thorough. Nations come to judgment on the field of battle. It is there that God decides which are fit to live and which must perish. War is a biological necessity. The warrior class constitutes the highest caste in the state. Since the men who use guns hold the chief place in the development of the world, they are to be held in exceptional honor. Among men of power they stand first, and to them must be given the first place in the hearts of their countrymen. This was the teaching of Treitschke. He said: " God will see to it that war always recurs as a drastic medicine for the human race." It was the conviction of Von Moltke. He said: " Perpetual peace is a dream, and not even a beautiful dream. But war is a link in the divine system of the universe." The militaristic philosophy has received its classic expression at the hands of General von Bernhardi. No writer in any country has ever stated the militarist position more clearly or with greater force. He boldly asserts that "war is the greatest factor in the furtherance of culture and power, a regulative element in the life of mankind which cannot be dispensed with. Without it a universal decadence would follow. Conquest is a law of necessity. The instinct of self preservation leads inevitably to war and the conquest of foreign soil."

But not all militarists belong to this extreme school. Many of them look upon war as an evil. It is a scourge to be dreaded. It is a cataclysm to be lamented. But it is impossible at all times to avoid it. It is a dark feature of the experience of a disordered world. As men are constituted, war is inevitable, and since wars are sure to recur, we must prepare for them. The preparation must be constant and efficacious. Military ef-

ficiency is one of a nation's most valuable as-
sets. By this efficiency she increases her
power for good in the world. By dominating
either the land or the sea or both, she renders
a service to humanity. By the influence of
guns she may become God's ordained peace-
maker among the nations. Armed peace is
the ideal, and the people which contributes
most generously to the maintenance of its
armament is the people which will do most
in the long run to ward off the dread affliction
of war. We have few Bernhardis, but
numerous militarists of the second grade.

Many militarists, however, refuse to go so
far as this. They hate war, and they are not
in love with armed peace. Nevertheless military preparedness, they think, is a national
duty. Nations must arm not to extend their
power, but solely in self defense. A nation
must fulfill its political obligations, and how
can it do this without a sufficient supply of
guns? Military discipline is on the whole
salutary. The drill which is given in the
army and navy contributes to physical health.

It builds up a manly carriage. It is also a factor in moral education. It teaches young men orderliness, and precision, and method, and best of all it trains them in obedience to authority. Before they enter the service they are slovenly and uncouth, they come out neat and self respecting, erect and obedient to superiors. Military and naval establishments are therefore worth all they cost. They are schools for educating the youth of the nation. They are seminaries for the inculcation of patriotism. They fit men for serving their country on the battlefield, should the nation be overtaken by the maelstrom of war. The boys of a nation should be trained to shoot. Target practice should have a place in the curriculum of the public school. Colleges should be centers for military training. A soldier nation is the ideal toward which we should strive. This is the type of militarist with whom we have to deal in this country.

All militarists then, however they may differ in details, agree on the exaltation of physical force. To a militarist the supreme national defense lies in material fortifications. Military power, he thinks, is supreme over all other forms of power. Military considerations are more weighty than all other considerations. The ultimate dependence of a nation must be upon its military strength.

Militarism may be defined, then, as being, first of all, a disposition, a temper, a spirit, a state of mind. It is a disposition to rely on physical forces, to magnify the importance of military equipment, a spirit of distrust in the power of ideas and ideals, of character and example, a state of mind in which one feels his nation to be in danger unless barricaded behind lines of bayonets and guns.

When this spirit works itself out into articulate expression, its creed runs somewhat as follows: "All life is foundationed on force. A nation is strong in proportion to its military defenses. Its prestige is to be computed in terms of naval tonnage. Its rank in the family of nations is fixed by the size of its army and fleet. Its dignity and influence are determined by the number and caliber of its guns. Its diplomats are forceful in international councils according to the number of bayonets behind them. It is absolutely at the mercy of any nation which possesses a completer military apparatus. National power is best symbolized by cannon. Practicing military maneuvers, preparing oneself to follow the flag to the battlefield is the surest evidence of exalted patriotism."

Out of the spirit comes a creed, and out of the creed come institutions — the army and the navy. These are visible, and therefore first catch the eye of the average man. To him they constitute what the world calls militarism. If they are colossal, he concludes that militarism is far advanced, if they are small, he decides that militarism is either nonexistent or as yet in the bud. He does not realize that " out of thought's interior sphere these wonders rose to upper air." Armies and navies are but exhalations rising from the surface of a state of mind. The vast armaments of the Christian world are tangible expressions of its materialism. They are incarnations of its appalling unbelief. Materialism has expressed itself in many forms, and militarism is its crowning and most amazing expression. The military equipment of the Christian world is its confession of unbelief in the potency of spiritual forces. A continent that weights itself with guns is really atheistic. It says by its action — no matter what it says with its tongue — there is no God, or if there is, he is Baal.

When, therefore, we come to grapple with militarism, it must not be forgotten that we are wrestling not against soldiers and sailors, but against the principalities, against the powers, against the world rulers of this darkness, against the spiritual hosts of wickedness in the heavenly places. The spirit of evil presents itself to our generation in its most formidable and most seductive incarnation, in that huge social phenomenon known as militarism. It is the greatest enemy of mankind which has thrown itself across the path of the world's forward march, since Martin Luther shattered the power of the mediæval priesthood. It is the most venomous and slimy reptile which has wound itself around the body of mankind since the serpent, slavery, was strangled. Like a modern Laocoon, the world writhes and groans in the crushing folds of this pitiless monster, and no one strong to save has yet appeared.

Pause a moment and glance at Europe as it was in the middle of July, 1914: The whole continent was at peace, and what a peace! It was an armed peace, the only kind of peace which militarism provides. Europe is nominally Christian. She is covered with cathedrals, but round her cathedrals there gleams the steel of her guns. She prays to a God of love, but through her streets continually there march battalions of armed men. She exalts Jesus of Nazareth to the right hand of God, but she trains her young men to fight sham battles outside the gates of all her cities. The land is covered with soldiers. Every soldier is drilling that he may become more expert in the taking of human life. And now look at the sea. It is covered with strange looking

vessels. What are they? They are dreadnoughts, and pre-dreadnoughts, and super-
dreadnoughts, and scout cruisers, and ar-
mored cruisers, and torpedo boats, and torpedo boat destroyers, and submarines. They
are filled with young men engaged in mock
battles, getting ready for the day when in real
battle they will send thousands of their fellow
beings to the bottom of the sea. And now
look into the air, another fleet, a navy of air
ships, what are they doing? Men in them are
practicing the art of dropping explosives, so
that when the next war comes, bombs can
be dropped successfully on women in their
beds, and little children in their cradles. And
all this in Christian Europe, in the continent
which has longest known of the life that was
lived in Galilee. All this in a time of peace,
when the masses of men and women desired
nothing so much as to be allowed to pursue
their work unmolested. Men on the land,
men on the water, men in the air, all drilling
that they might be ready for the next war.
Who set them to doing this? Militarists —

three classes of them — first, men who were believers in war, and second, men who hated war but believed in armed peace, and third, men who lamented the expensiveness of armed peace, but who believed it to be wise to train each new generation of boys to shoot. And all this nineteen hundred years after Jesus died on the cross!

And so, for decades, Europe has been the scandal and shame of the world. She has retarded the progress of Christianity in every part of the non-Christian world. The oriental eye caught the gleam of her bayonets before it caught the glimmer of her church spires, and when the East sent West for helpers, it was not for ministers of the Gospel, but for generals and admirals who might teach the boys of Asia how best to destroy human life.

It is needless to dwell upon the unspeakable tragedy. We call the war tragic, and so it is, but Europe has known nothing but tragedy for many a year. Is it not tragic to see Christian nations squandering their treasure in implements of blood, while millions of their people toil in poverty, denied all the luxuries and many of them even the necessaries of life? Is it not tragic when nations spend on guns what they ought to spend on the education of their people? Is it not tragic when government deliberately puts a soldier on the back of every peasant, and compels him to carry that soldier until his strength fails, and he falls into the grave? Is it not tragic to see so-called Christian statesmen turning each year the screws of taxation a little tighter, rolling up the national debt a little larger, not because humanitarian projects are being carried forward, but solely because it is deemed necessary to lay in a still larger stock of ammunition and guns? Is it not tragic that the two leading Christian nations of the world have for many years been running a race in naval expansion, and that other nations, including our own, have endeavored to keep up with the procession? Is it not tragic to hear men who profess allegiance to Jesus Christ talking about, " dominion," " control," " domination," words which the Son of God never used, and against whose use he uttered solemn warnings? Did he not say: "Ye know that the princes of the nations exercise dominion over them, and they that are great exercise authority upon them? But it shall not be so among you, but whosoever will be great among you, let him be your minister, and whosoever will be chief among you, let him be your servant." Will not that command remain after the sun has gone out, and the heavens have been rolled together as a scroll? What robberies there have been both in Asia and in Africa, the robber in every case carrying off his booty because he was supplied with guns. And what diabolical talk there has been, talk of "blood and iron," and "shining armor" and "rattling sabers," and "bleeding a nation white," and "beating a nation to her knees," and "crushing a nation so that never again would she cross her neighbor's path." All this in Christian Europe! How different it sounds from those words repeated long ago, and which are law for all the nations to the

end of time: "Love your enemies. Bless
them that curse you, do good to them that
hate you, and pray for them that despitefully
use you." Over the whole history of modern Europe you may write the word tragedy.
The war is only another chapter of a dolorous
story, a little more pathetic and heart breaking than the chapter that preceded it. No
continent can write the first chapter without
being compelled to go on and write the second.
Nations which sow bayonets reap battles.
Peoples who prepare for fighting come to
blows. Kings who revel in guns fill their
land with graves.

Militarism is the root cause of the great
war. The war was precipitated by small
cliques of blind and narrow-headed men who
were educated in the camp of Cæsar. The
generals and admirals were packed close
around the thrones of Austria and Germany
and Russia, and the war was declared by men
who have eyes for nothing but military necessities. It is these men and men like them in
France and Great Britain who have dragged

Europe to perdition. It is because of them
that European diplomacy has long been nothing but a cover for robbery. Reputable statesmen skulk in the dark, making alliances and
ententes which they do not dare to explain to
the people. The habits of many of the
diplomats of Europe have long been the
habits of bandits and cut-throats. No wonder
God said at last: " The measure of your in-
iquity is full." The war is heaven's retribu-
tion on Europe's sins.

Militarism, or the trust in physical force,
always works by means of fear, and fear has
torments. Militarism begins with a false assumption. It says to nations: " You are
natural enemies of one another, and being
enemies, you ought to distrust and suspect
one another." That is the greatest lie the
devil has told since he lied to the first man
in Eden. " Since you cannot trust one another, you must arm yourselves against one
another, and the more complete your equipment the more likely you are to escape harm."
And thus the arming began. One nation

armed, and its neighbor immediately followed
its example, other neighbors in turn coming
soon after into the same demoralizing game.
It was thus that all Europe became in time
an armed camp. Each nation strove for the
highest possible efficiency. Each was fearful
that some other nation might get the advantage
of it. Slight suspicions led to fears, and out
of the fears came a system of espionage whose
blighting and defiling touch has been on all
European life. Nations became feverishly
anxious to know what their neighbors were
doing. When we measure ourselves against
others by the standards of physical force, it
is important that we should know the nature
of the latest explosive and the caliber of the
very last gun. Europe has swarmed for years
with spies, and the spies created fresh rumors
and additional alarms. Once terrorized, the
nations became still more zealous in making
their salvation sure. They increased their
battalions, they added more ships of war.
They began to spy on one another from Zeppelins and aëroplanes. They became increas-

ingly nervous, agitated, excited. Now and then they fell into a sort of hysteria. They were harassed by hallucinations. They were tortured by imaginary goblins and monsters. At last they came to have all the symptoms of insanity. They agonized in a kind of delirium tremens. More than once within the last ten years England has been crazy. So also has France. So also has Germany. It is a singular fact that the nations most heavily armed are the ones which suffer most from this exhausting delirium. Germany especially became so excitable that she peopled the world with specters. It was the Kaiser who coined the phrase: "The Yellow Peril." The German General Staff always saw Germany girt with a ring of foes. On the first of August Germany was so beside herself she could not wait until Russia declared war on her, she was so wild that she could not wait even to keep her treaty obligations with Belgium. It all seems so strange to us who are on the outside, for it is difficult to see why Germany, with her magnificent army, should have been so

frightened by her alleged enemies, and why
with all her wonderful siege guns and her
matchless submarines, and her astounding
Zeppelins, and her intrepid battalions she
should feel it necessary to run the risk of losing Italy's help by declaring war on Russia,
and England's neutrality by invading Belgium.
There is no explanation of her conduct except
that she was driven forward by a blind and
irrational fear. The war was precipitated by
an abnormal reaction of the German mind to
a situation which she had done more than
anybody else to create. It is fear then
that has created the entanglements out of
which the war of ten nations developed.
Fear was the cause of the dual alliance, and
fear was responsible for the triple alliance,
and fear was also the father of the triple
entente. The present war is, as the Crown
Prince of Germany says, utterly stupid and
inexcusable. The nations are fighting simply
because they are afraid of one another.
They became afraid of one another because
they were all armed to the teeth. When na-

tions are liberally supplied with 42-centimeter howitzers, and rapid-firing machine guns, and ubiquitous submarines, and bomb dropping aëroplanes, they do well to be afraid of one another. Fear hath torments. Fear is hell. Love only can cast out fear, and love is a word which militarism does not know. Militarism understands compulsion, not persuasion; coercion, not wooing; crushing, not affection; Cæsar, not Christ. Militarism has brought Europe into the abyss, the question now is, will the new world take warning from the old, or will the new world pattern after the example of the old, and rush by and by to a similar destruction? Every nation which surrenders to militarism is doomed.

Is there any danger that the United States may ever suffer from the blight of militarism? The usual answer is, " No." A member of the Cabinet said the other day: " No reasonable person in this country has the slightest shadow of fear of military despotism, nor of any interference whatever by military force in the conduct of civil affairs." This is no doubt the general feeling. "Look at our little army," men say, "and look at our third rate navy, and note the temper of our people! Our republic is in no danger of becoming infected by the militarist bacillus. Our greatest men have all abhorred war. Our greatest general said: 'Let us have peace.' The traditions of the country are all for peace. Why should any one be alarmed?"

But there are certain facts which ought not to be blinked. The world is to-day organically one. All the nations are united. It is impossible for any one of them to be afflicted with any disease, without all of the rest of them taking in more or less of the poison. Nations, like children, catch diseases by being thrown in with those who are sick. When contagion is in the air, and all nations are exposed to breezes which blow round the world, it is not wise to be too certain that a European fever might not also some day burn in our own blood.

It is true that our army and navy are not at all likely to interfere, openly, to-day or to-

morrow, in the conduct of civil affairs, but
they certainly have more influence on national policy than they had forty years ago,
and the number of Americans who make a
fetish of military preparedness is growing
year by year. The expansion of the United
States navy within the last thirty years is one
of the outstanding phenomena of our history.
In 1881 our navy cost us only $13,000,000. In
1891 it cost us only $22,000,000. In the next
ten years the cost went up to $56,000,000. By
1911 it had reached $121,000,000. Two years
later it had mounted to $146,000,000. And
this year the government is asking for $148-
589,786. But according to the plans of the
Naval Board our navy is yet but a baby.
Every naval expert confesses that it is totally
inadequate to our needs. We have only fifteen dreadnoughts, whereas we must have at
the lowest, forty-eight, and one rear-admiral
has suggested that we ought to have eighty.
The navy has been pushed ahead rather than
the army because of our extensive coastline,
and because of the example of Great Britain

and Germany, and also because it is easier
to show off a navy than it is to show off an
army. It is impossible to bring the army to
New York City every year, whereas it is easy
to exhibit the navy in the Hudson River,
where the New York reporters can see it, and
blow its praises across the continent. But the
army is not without its ambitions and hopes.
It expects to expand later on. The military
experts have told us a thousand times that our
present army is scandalously insignificant, and
must be multiplied by two or three, and later
on by five. The general staff worked out
plans three years ago for an army of 500,000.
Last year the army cost us $94,000,000. Next
year it is to cost us $106,000,000. And this
does not include the cost of fortifications and
other things which an army must have. So
that to-day we are spending over $250,000,000
a year for military purposes, far more than
we are spending for anything else. Did you
notice the items in the national budget recently laid before Congress. We are asked
to spend this next year:

On our Judicial Establishment...........$ 1,240,000
On Foreign Intercourse.................. 4,607,000
On the Legislative Establishment........ 7,641,000
On Indian Affairs....................... 9,533,000
On the Panama Canal.................... 19,000,000
On the Department of Agriculture....... 20,706,000
On the Executive Establishment......... 31,846,000

Or a total of.......................$94,573,000

Not so much on seven great departments of our government as on our army establishment alone. And if to the army appropriation you add that for the navy, you use up a considerable part of all our income. So that we are handicapped in all our efforts to do constructive work for the social and industrial betterment of our people. When we ought to be spending scores of millions of dollars on our roads and canals, on our deserts and swamps, on our farms and public buildings, and when we ought to be increasing the number of our Federal Judges, and paying our Ambassadors adequate salaries, and erecting in every foreign capital an ambassador's residence which would be an honor to our republic, and entering upon a national campaign for educating the negroes of the South, and for stamping out tuberculosis throughout the country, and for strengthening the agencies for increasing the health and happiness of our people, we are already, in time of peace, spending a quarter of a billion dollars every year upon our army and navy, and this is a mere bagatelle compared with what the military and naval experts want to spend. And so while, in one sense, it is true that militarism is not yet interfering in the conduct of the civil affairs of this country, in another sense it is profoundly modifying the whole policy of our government. Congress is giving more and more time to the discussion of military matters, and more and more of our national income is being expended each year on the instruments of war.

If you ask why Congress is willing to cripple the civil departments of the government for the aggrandisement of the naval establishment, the answer is that Congress is responsive to an unhealthy public sentiment which

has been created by the propaganda carried
on for a generation by a company of astute
and determined men. The nation has been
sent to school and the rising generation has
been taught lessons that our fathers never
learned. The same tactics are used in this
country which have proved successful across
the sea. Admiral Von Tirpitz built up the
German navy by means of a Navy League.
Such a league has been established in our national capital. As a New York paper said
the other day: "It numbers in its member-
ship a great many well known men." That is
the method of all Navy Leagues. They en-
roll many "well known men." Illustrious
names carry influence. Men not ˈso well
known, behind this influence, can do the work.
It would be impossible to say just how much
of the propaganda for military preparedness
in this country can be traced to the Navy
League, but we know that throughout the
country systematic and effective work is being done for an ever bigger navy. For in-

stance, the battleships are named after the different states, to stir up in each state a public enthusiasm over increased naval appropriations. Battleships are launched with great éclat, all the leading state officials, and as many of the national officials as possible being present. There is an annual review of ships of war in the Hudson River that city crowds may clap their hands over them, and young women of prominent families may examine and admire the guns — and the men — and the newspapers may advertise the needs of the navy to every other newspaper throughout the land. We have our annual war scares after the approved European fashion. We have nervous citizens writing letters to the newspapers, calling attention to the imminent danger of foreign attack. Generals and admirals give interviews to enterprising reporters, the burden of their story always being our frightful unpreparedness. Captains and commodores write for the Sunday papers, and, when gifted with a golden mouth, they make after dinner speeches, while retired rear-admirals write books or stump the country in the interests of an ever enlarging fleet.

In our country as in Europe, the appeal is always to one's fears. It is by fear that militarism does its mighty works. Congress pours out the money for additional battleships because Congress is made afraid. It is afraid that Japan is going to steal the Philippines! There has been for several years a planned propaganda in this country to misrepresent Japan, and to inflame American feeling against her. Faked interviews are published from time to time in papers counted respectable, purporting to give alarmist opinions of distinguished men, the interviews being denied two or three days later. Congress is afraid that Germany is going to annex Brazil, or some other section of South America, thus trampling on the Monroe doctrine. There is a sinister propaganda to keep that fear alive. If you will watch the movements of a militarist, you will find he invariably appeals to fear. A naval architect tells how readily a foreign power could take possession of Boston, New York and Philadelphia. An inventor of guns startles an audience by reminding it of our shortage in powder. A retired captain of the navy writes in a Sunday paper that it is chimerical to think that wars will ever cease to be waged. He remembers that Christ drove the money changers out of the temple, and frankly admits that " it might not prove altogether a misfortune to have a war forced upon us in the near future." An ex-president of the United States in order to create a still wilder alarm, confides to an audience that he has seen with his own eyes plans formed by two foreign nations for the invasion of our country. The letters published in the papers on military and naval matters are interesting. They are written largely by men who have been terrorized. One says that our navy is absurdly insufficient to protect our coasts, another says that our homes and wealth and pride are in imminent jeopardy. Another asserts that we are treading in the paths of decadent nations. Another hysterically begs

Congress to make haste, because there is not an hour to be lost. Whoever feeds the fires of fear, makes it easier for militarists to work their will. The present war has increased the fear of all our militarists. They are in a state of frenzied consternation. A United States Senator declares that public buildings must wait. We must have more ships, and he does not care what they cost. A Congressman after talking with a few army and naval officers, utters so shrill a shriek that it is reported all over the land. A college president falls suddenly in love with the Swiss system of military drill, and wants ours to become a soldier-nation.

The present agitation for increased military preparedness has brought out certain facts which ought not to be overlooked. It appears that we have a shocking scarcity of auxiliary vessels in the navy. Our costly dreadnoughts are comparatively worthless, because we have not the needed ships to protect them. We have, moreover, many battleships, but we have not enough men to man them.

At the lowest estimate over five thousand men are lacking in the Atlantic fleet. We have excellent coast guns, but we have not the men to fire them. We have more guns than powder. In an hour or two our whole stock of powder would be exhausted. It is when we consider facts like these that we see militarism on its seamiest side. The Secretary of War tells us that a large proportion of the army posts are worthless. The Secretary of the Navy assures us that a large number of the navy yards are needless. The men at the head of affairs confess to us that after all our lavish expenditure of money, and after these years of toil in getting ready, we are in a condition of pitiable helplessness, absolutely at the mercy of any foe who cares to strike. Why do you suppose dreadnoughts are built out of all proportion to auxiliary vessels? Is it because the profit on big ships is greater? And why do we go on building more ships, when we do not have the men to man the ships we already have? Is it because somebody is pushing harder for ships than somebody else is push-

ing for men? Why do we buy more guns
when we lack men to fire the guns we have?
Can it be that there is more profit in guns
than in men? Why do we go on ordering
guns, when we lack the powder to make them
effective? Is it because guns cost more
money than powder, and because it is more
profitable to deal in one rather than in the
other? What kind of men have we had in
Washington City the last twenty years, that
things should get into this disgraceful predicament? If half that has been said within the
last thirty days about the condition of our
army and navy is true, then the men who
have been in authority in Washington City
are branded with ineffaceable disgrace. What
is the use of going on squandering our
money for preparation, to find ourselves at
last totally unprepared? Militarism whets
the appetite of war traders and increases the
number and importunacy of the lobbyists, and
opens up numberless new avenues for graft
and jobbery, and every sort of political corruption. For many reasons, Americans have

more cause to be on their guard against militarists than against any other class of our people. As soon as a nation is swayed by fear, it abdicates the throne of reason, and is ready to plunge into all sorts of wild and destructive excesses.

A word of caution at this point is necessary. Because militarists are dangerous, it does not follow that every man in the United States army and navy is dangerous. Not every man in our army and navy is a militarist. Many of them are not. Many are noble and sensible and peace loving men. Many of them refuse to run to Congress for additional legislation, and to sell themselves to the Sunday newspapers, and to talk at every opportunity with newspaper reporters, and to stump the country to extend the reign of fear. Many have never been Prussianized, and refuse to subscribe to the militarist creed. For these men let us have nothing but respect and gratitude. We cannot get on as a nation without an army and a navy for police purposes, and consequently to hold a place in either of them is both honorable and Christian. There is no reason why any Christian man should on account of his religion, refuse to enter either service. There is work of many kinds which trained soldiers can do better than anybody else. What Americans stand higher to-day in the esteem of us all than Col. Goethals and Col. Gorgas? They are only specimens of a fine body of men of whom we Americans have every reason to be proud. But in our army and navy there are also dangerous men, dangerous because dominated by false ideas, and because in the enthusiasm of their pagan faith, they are ready to move heaven and earth to bring this nation down to the low level of Europe. Whenever they write or speak they make mischief because they exploit mistaken ideals. Experts in military maneuvers, they know nothing of statesmanship or the moral order of the world. They look at everything through the bore of a gun, and they bring down the ideals of every young man whom they touch. It was this type of man who poisoned the brain and heart of Europe and who more than anybody else is responsible for the great war.

Let us not be deceived by loud talk about our unpreparedness. It is our good fortune that we are unprepared. Do not let us be ashamed of our little army. Its diminutive size is a crown of glory. How proud we should feel that we have the smallest army of any great power in the world. Let us not shed tears when our navy slips down from second place to third place, and let us not be in terror if it slips from third place into fourth, and from fourth into fifth. It is not a disgrace to be the lowest in the list. It is possible that in this as in certain other things, to be first is to be last, and to be last is to be first.

Let us beware of coveting military efficiency. The first effect of it would be to make nations afraid of us. It is the worst fate which can befall a nation, that other nations become afraid of it. Fear passes inevitably into hate, and the hate of its neighbors is the one thing which no nation can afford. We have enough unfortunate handi-

caps already without adding another. We
are large. We have an immense country,
with a vast population and with enormous resources. We have a tendency to brag and to
strut. We let the American Eagle scream too
much. We are commercially ambitious and
aggressive and pushing, and a complete suit of
armor would only intensify our native traits.
We are an inflammable people. We have
great cities which readily catch fire. We have
demagogues in Congress, and jingoes in possession of some of our papers. It was not
many years ago that in many of our cities mobs
cried out like wild Indians: " Remember the
Maine!" We cannot afford to run the risk
of being prepared. It would be dangerous
for us to be able to strike at the drop of the
hat. We never want to be able to issue ultimatums. We do not desire our government
to be geared up for war. We must keep it in
a condition of unpreparedness to shed blood.
It was the preparedness of Europe which
pushed it over the precipice into the abyss.
Had it not been so completely prepared for

battle, there would have been time for the exercise of reason. Reason was absolutely banished by Europe's preparedness for war. They say it would take us months to get ready to meet a foe. This is our safeguard. While we are getting ready we shall have time to talk with our enemy, and after a good frank conference, a way out of the difficulty is likely to emerge.

Because of our size and our resources and our temper, any conspicuous and exaggerated preparedness on our part only excites irritation in smaller nations, and increases their dislike of us. We cannot add to our military and naval equipment without stirring fears and unfriendly feelings in the hearts of the South American peoples. They are afraid of us already, and every new battleship we build only makes them still more afraid. Mr. Bryce has told us that they are far more afraid of us than they are of the Germans. We, at the same time, by every addition to our navy, increase Japan's fear of us. We have taken Hawaii, and the Philippines, and there

are men in Japan foolish enough to think that
our next move will be to take Japan. This
sounds like lunacy to you, but why should that
be counted insane, when we have honorable
men in this country not in an insane asylum
but in high positions who believe that Japan
at the first opportunity will attack and try to
humble the United States?

Every move in increased armament by us
has its effect on every European nation.
Great Britain and Germany count the number of our dreadnoughts as carefully as they
count their own, and naval policy on the other
side of the Atlantic will always be influenced
by what our policy is.

For the sake of the world, then, as well as
for our own sake, we cannot afford to go on
building an ever bigger navy, or begin to
agitate for the doubling of our army. Our
only hope of leading the nations out of the
present dilemma is to set them an example.
We cannot expect them to lay down their
arms so long as we are buying new ones. Our
Secretary of the Navy hopes the day will come

when the feverish haste and competition in costly engines of destruction will stop, but he goes right on recommending new battleships and submarines for the United States Navy. He says the American people are against making the United States into a military nation in competition with the heavily armed powers of Europe, and in the next breath he says that the American navy should be steadily strengthened. A man who talks thus has never thought this subject through. If we are not going to compete with European nations in armament then we must cease buying armor. If we want the feverish competition to stop, we must first stop ourselves. Do you suppose we can disarm Europe by bluster? Can we woo her from her false policies by fear? Never. It was the sun and not the wind which induced the traveler to take off his coat. Only a nation unarmed can induce another nation to believe in disarmament. But would it not be a risk for the United States to cease to buy guns? Of course it would. But to take risks is a thing which America was ordained to do. It took a risk when it abolished kings, and another risk when it dispensed with a state church, and another risk when it trusted everything to the people, and another risk when it admitted foreigners from all countries, and another risk when it decided to leave its northern boundary of thirty-eight hundred miles without a fort. These are all colossal risks, but what else besides these have we done that is really glorious? Nothing truly great can be done in this world which is not a risk. It is only great men and great nations which throw themselves into hazardous ventures. It is only by a magnificent act of heroism that America can cut the chain by which the nations now are bound. Why should not America risk its life, if necessary, in order to save the world?

Militarism and Christianity are implacable and irreconcilable foes. The one believes in the mailed fist, the other trusts the power of the hand that is pierced. The one worships the big stick, the other commits all things to the heart that is gentle. The one declares that might makes right, the other believes that right makes might. The one believes that the strong can conquer the weak, the other believes that the weak can conquer the strong. The one works by fear, the other works by persuasion. The one asserts that the foundation of the universe is force, the other declares that the universe is built on love. Militarism is from beneath, Christianity is from above. Militarism is materialism in its deadliest manifestation. It is atheism in its most brutal and blatant incarnation. It is the enemy of God and man. It must be overthrown. Every nation which embraces it goes down to the chambers of death.

By its fruits we are to judge it. Militarism generates an evil spirit in the hearts of men. It feeds suspicion, and distrust, and hate. It sows the seed of dissension, and fills the world with disquieting rumors. It is the arch deceiver. It promises nations safety, insurance, guarantees of peace, and then overwhelms them in a sea of blood. It keeps humanity back from attaining its goal. All the peoples of Europe wanted peace, and so — I think — did all the rulers, but it was not possible for rulers or peoples to secure what they desired, because Europe was held tight in the clutches of a set of militarist oligarchies.

Militarism offers no hope for the future. When it looks ahead it sees nothing but carnage. At the end of this war America must prepare to fight the victor — so our militarists are saying. Later on there will be a great conflict between the Anglo-Saxon and the Slav, and after that there will come a world shattering clash between the Orient and the West. Through the centuries there will be suspicion and hatred, increasing taxation and suffering, and labor and anguish, and the end of it all a bloody tomb! Such a philosophy of life must have been formulated in hell. It is only in hell that men abandon hope. Militarists are tortured with fears for the present, and beyond them there rise no delectable mountains aglow with the glory of God.

But when we turn to Christianity she speaks to us with a soothing, healing accent. She uses the vocabulary of consolation. She bids us to have faith, and she exhorts us to hope, and she tells us of the wonder and power of love. She speaks to us of a Father in Heaven who loves all his children, and of a race of men all of whom are brothers, and she pictures for us a beautiful world — far off in the future — in which nations learn war no more. Those who listen to her find themselves delivered from a great bondage, and in newness of heart they go out saying to everybody: " God has not given us the spirit of fear, but of power, and of love, and of a sound mind."

V

Fallacies of Militarism

ERROR never walks naked across the earth. It always puts on robes which make it look like the truth. The spirit of evil never approaches us with hoofs and horns, but always as an angel of light. Militarism has gotten its tenacious grip on the world by the use of the magic of delusive words. Its power lies in the sophistries which it proclaims as incontrovertible axioms. It works its will by putting out men's eyes, and it puts out men's eyes by throwing into them the acid of beliefs that are false.

Militarists of all countries work after the same fashion in winning new converts and extending their power. They begin by discrediting the men who oppose them. They call them sentimentalists, visionaries, utopians, dreamers. They accuse them of being ignorant of human nature. They do not know, they say, the nature of man, or heed the lessons of human experience. They are unacquainted with the conditions which exist in our modern world, theirs is the valor of ignorance. Sometimes the accusation becomes harsher. These pacifists are called peace-at-any-price men, that is, men who are willing to lie down and be trampled on, and who advise nations to submit meekly to every outrage which may be perpetrated on them. Peace-at-any-price men have no sense of honor, nor are they loyal to the principles of righteousness. They put tranquillity above righteousness, and freedom from pain above justice. They care nothing for principle, if only they can save their skin. For instance, a distinguished editor of a reputable weekly says, " We believe that those who seek international righteousness *through national impotence* are brothers to those who might hope to abolish individual murder by abolishing the civil police." The assumption is that without colossal armies and navies nations are impotent, and that the only way of securing righteousness on the earth is through preparedness to indulge on a great scale in human slaughter. To make the pacifists look ignorant, silly, and ridiculous is the first move always in the militarist campaign. If you can create the impression that any set of men are lacking not only in patriotism but also in genuine devotion to high principle of any sort, you have gone a long way in breaking the force of their arguments.

This charge of ignorance is a subtle one, and how to answer it is not, to many, at once apparent. When men say that only the military and naval experts are competent to pass judgment on matters relating to the national defense, and that we shall do wisely to allow the specialists to determine for us what our national policy shall be, there is a plausibility in the assertion which is captivating, and likely to be convincing unless one looks into the claim and separates the truth in it from the falsehood. It is true that in all technical matters in the art of war, we must defer to the judgment of our military experts. They are the only men who can tell us how mines are to be laid, and how they can be swept up, how far projectiles can be hurled, and how much damage explosives will do, how thick the armor plate on the battleships shall be, and of what material the strongest fortifications are built. Within his own province, the military expert is supreme. He alone possesses the technical knowledge which is able to solve the problems which modern warfare presents. But outside of this narrow circle of technical knowledge, the military expert is not to be accepted as an oracle. The very fact that he is a specialist devoting his life to one narrow range of data should make us wary of trusting him in the larger field of statesmanship. The study of projectiles and explosives does not of necessity unfold the mind for dealing with the problems which international life presents. Target practice on the land or sea does not train the eye to see the great facts of life as they are. Pondering the history of military campaigns, and mapping imaginary battlefields is not ideal training for men who are to guide the feet of nations into the paths of peace. It is a mischievous assumption that army and navy officers have peculiar qualifications for dealing with the problems of statesmanship, and that they, more than all others, are to be consulted in determining the policy and program of a nation in the realm of international relations. It is a trick of all oligarchies to gather up power into their own hands. Military cliques have a swift way of determining what are military necessities. They trample without mercy on men who stand in their way. They are the last men in the nation to be consulted on the large questions of national policy, and expenditures. We are a democracy, and no man of us can for a moment consent to stand dumb on the most critical and far-reaching of all national problems, allowing leadership to pass into the hands of a special caste. Every American citizen of intelligence and

conscience is competent to form opinions as to
the right relation of our nation to the other
nations of the earth, and to reach conclusions
as to the amount of money which we can
wisely spend each year on guns. One need
not be an expert on the comparative value of
submarines and dreadnoughts, or on the explosive powers of lyddite and melinite, in
order to take intelligent part in the discussion
of the great question of national defense. A
man who is tolerably well acquainted with the
history of the last two thousand years, and
who is conversant with the principles laid
down in the New Testament, is better fitted
to deal with these high matters than any
number of men whose chief claim to distinction is a knowledge of the chemistry of explosives, and a mastery of the tactics of war.
Thousands of our fellow citizens are quite too
humble. They have allowed themselves to be
browbeaten by military and naval nabobs.
They have come to look upon the questions
clustering round army and navy as remote
from them, matters in which they are not to

interfere.   It is only by getting all classes of the people to think and talk of these matters, that the power of the militarist can be broken.

Sometimes every effort to get the world into a different mood and practice is discouraged on the ground that all such efforts are hopeless.   " Human nature is what it is, and cannot be changed.   Men have always fought, and therefore they always will fight.   There have been wars from the beginning, and therefore there will be wars to the end.   They are forever inevitable, and consequently our only wise course is to prepare for them."

The argument seems at first not only plausible but unanswerable.   There is no doubt that man from the beginning has been a belligerent creature, and that war has continued with only brief interruptions up to the present hour.   It cannot be denied that neither science nor art nor religion nor law has been able to abolish it, and that it is now raging in its most horrible and devastating form.   If we are to judge of the future by the past, it would seem that we must accept what the militarist says.

But it is not true that man cannot be changed. Science will not permit us to say that. Science holds the theory of evolution, and contends that the whole universe of life is going on and up. It says that the horse has changed, and that the dog has evolved. It declares that herbs and flowers and trees have all passed through transformations, and that by pressure exerted by man, these transformations can be accelerated and guided. Science has carefully gathered up the relics of primitive man, and takes delight in pointing out how he has been slowly climbing on stepping stones of his dead self to higher things. It seems singular that any man who has breathed the atmosphere of the modern scientific world should ever say a thing so stupid as that man cannot be changed. He is the one creature among all the animals on our planet who is most susceptible to change. He can be changed more rapidly and more radically

than any other living being. If this were not
true, all educators would be discouraged, and
all religious teachers would work in vain.

History declares on every page that human
nature can be changed. You cannot change
the constitution of the human mind or the
corpuscles in the human blood, but you can
change man's ideals, his beliefs, his desires,
and changing these, you change his conduct,
and when you change his conduct you change
the world. Because a thing has existed for centuries it does not follow that it must always be.
Slavery existed for uncounted thousands of
years. There never lived a Greek or Roman
who dared to dream that it would ever cease
to be. It lived on century after century even
in countries which confessed allegiance to
Jesus of Nazareth. In our own country it
died only about fifty years ago. After con-
tinuing for thousands of generations it finally
vanished, and no one believes it will ever come
back again.

For millenniums men believed in witchcraft.
It was not an isolated belief, it was universal.

It was not temporary, but persistent. It held its grip upon the mind for ages. Less than two hundred years ago, all the most learned and most highly cultivated men upon the earth believed in the power of witches, and it is said that in the seventeenth century in Europe alone over one hundred thousand men and women were put to death on the charge of being guilty of this awful crime. Men living in that century no doubt were certain that the belief in witchcraft would abide forever, and yet in less than two hundred years it has vanished completely from all civilized countries, and will never come back again. As soon as men ceased to believe in witchcraft, they ceased to kill women on the charge of being witches.

For centuries the courts of Europe in order to find out the guilt of prisoners subjected them to various forms of torture. It was a clumsy and cruel procedure, and yet it was sanctioned by the highest legal authorities in the world. Instruments of torture used in the mediæval ages are on exhibition in all the museums of Europe, and we look upon them with wonder and horror. As soon as men came to believe that the truth can be ascertained more surely in other ways than by the use of torture, the old instruments were laid aside.

Now suppose that men should some day cease to believe in war as the best way of settling international disputes, just as they have ceased to believe in witchcraft, and in slavery and in the use of torture, then the making of guns would cease. That such a time will come is as certain as it is that slavery is dead. Victor Hugo spoke with the insight of a prophet when years ago he declared that the time would come when a cannon ball would be preserved in museums, to be looked at with the same feelings with which we now gaze on the abandoned instruments of torture.

Science and history thus combine to repudiate the assertion that human nature cannot be changed, and in this they are supported by religion. Christianity is the religion that goes the farthest in its belief in the changeable-

ness of man. It assumes that he can be
changed, not superficially but radically. Not
only can his ideals and beliefs be altered, but
he can be transformed down to the very roots
of his being. He can be born again. Not
only is this possible, but it is a necessity. A
man must be born again in order to enter into
the kingdom of God. A man's disposition, attitude, affections, all can be changed and must
be changed, this is fundamental in the religion
of Jesus. How can a Christian with the New
Testament before him ever admit that human
nature cannot be changed? Man can be mar-
velously transformed in the course of a few
centuries. Our forefathers drank blood out
of the skulls of their murdered foes, and to
do that again in the hall of Valhalla was their
highest conception of heaven. We have been
changed from character to character by the
working of the spirit of the Lord. But men
can be changed in one generation. When
John G. Paton went to the New Hebrides he
found only degraded and murderous canni-
bals. Before he laid down his work, thou-

sands of men and women, once savages, were singing in happy Christian homes the praises of God.

It is only when you have disposed of the fallacy of the alleged unchangeableness of human nature, that you can successfully deal with another of the most seductive of the militarist fallacies: " In time of peace prepare for war." It is a pagan adage, born in a world into which Jesus had not yet come, and it was repeated with approbation by good men down to the days of Washington, just as the belief in witchcraft survived down to the days of John Wesley. Washington accepted it just as Wesley accepted the belief in witches. But there are men who would keep it alive forever. Even in the twentieth century they think it wise to make this old outworn adage the basis of national policy.

It is a maxim which belonged primarily to a world of savages. When Columbus discovered America he found the natives had reached that stage of development in which it was necessary in time of peace to prepare for war. War was the established occupation of all the tribes. Men lived to fight. Now and then there came a lull in the fighting, and in that lull it was necessary to provide new tomahawks and additional arrows for the battle which was certain soon to begin. So long as men are savages there is nothing for them to do but to prepare for war in time of peace. The adage is also workable among barbarians, and even among semi-barbarians, and that was as high as most peoples rose before the Christian era. Roman history, for instance, from Romulus to Cæsar Augustus is a history of war. In the entire period of seven hundred years there were only brief and scattered seasons of peace. It was counted heroic to kill men, and greatness was measured by the extent of the slaughter. But with the advent of Christianity, there came a change in the ideals and sentiments of men, and war began to lose some of its ancient glory. Little by little, very slowly, the ideals of peace have made progress against the ideals of war, until now, although wars still occur, they are looked upon by all good men with horror. In savage lands men fight all the time: in barbaric countries they fight most of their time, in semi-civilized countries they fight much of their time, but in Christianized countries they now fight only a little of their time. Peace is now the normal state of mankind, and war is abnormal. No sooner does a war now begin than a vast multitude of people begin at once to hope and plan for its ending. War is something which has become abhorrent and well-nigh unendurable. Wars are now therefore only occasional. When they occur, they so break up all the arrangements of our life, that they seem to be incursions from some infernal world. When nations lived isolated lives, and modern commerce had not yet been born, and none of the thousand tender ties by which we are now bound together had been formed, war was not a world wide calamity. But now no two nations can fight without all nations suffering with them. War breaks down the machinery of the world, it upsets all the normal processes of living and working, it stabs humanity in the heart. Wars have become so expensive and exhausting that they cannot come often. They will come less frequently in the future than they came in the past. The periods of peace will gradually increase. The duration of war will gradually shorten. And now in these changed conditions to go on saying: " In time of peace prepare for war," is to talk like a parrot that repeats something not because it is sensible or pertinent but because it has been said. To spend the long years of peace in drilling for a few months of war, to pile up through decades of peace, apparatus and ammunition which can be used up in one short and furious and deadly struggle, certainly that is the advice of men who have lost their senses. They have become obsessed by an ancient adage. " New occasions teach new duties, time makes ancient good uncouth." The adage for our age is: " In time of peace, prepare for a longer and a richer and a more stable peace. Get your peace machinery in order. Have the wheels of the peace machine oiled so that they will turn easily when the hour of crisis comes. Clashes of interest there will always be, outbursts of passion there will always be, temptations to overreach and to strike there will always be, and so you must prepare for the perilous hour, and have your house so completely in order that when international relations become strained, and passions which are divisive become mighty, you shall have ready to your hand, the legal instruments which will enable you to curb the turbulent elements and keep the arbitrament of reason supreme."

It used to be said that preparedness for war is the only sure guarantee of peace. A monstrous fallacy, and yet almost universally accepted. It was on this plea that European nations armed themselves to the teeth. They were willing to bring themselves to the verge of bankruptcy if only they could escape the horror and ruin of war. But their efforts were vain. The very means selected to avert an unspeakable calamity proved to be the most efficacious instrument for bringing it on. Men no longer say that preparedness is the *only* guarantee of peace; they now affirm that it is the *surest* guarantee of peace. If this is so, then we have no guarantees of peace which are of the slightest value. Two nations of Europe which were the most thoroughly prepared — Russia and Germany — are the two nations which clashed the soonest. Where the armies were largest, there was most talk of an alleged inevitable conflict. The German has long looked upon war with the Slav as unescapable, and the Slav has considered the Teuton as a foe certainly to be reckoned with. The larger the armies became the stronger grew the conviction that war was inevitable. Nations cannot bend their energies to preparations for war without ultimately fighting. The things we prepare for are the things which we get. The seeds that we sow are certain to come up. Standing armies will stand for a season, but soon or late they grow impatient and move. Playing at war is fascinating for a time, but grown-up men after awhile grow weary of it, and long to live in earnest. Sham battles on land and sea never satisfy. They always leave undemonstrated what the military experts most of all want to know. It is only in the fiery furnace of battle that the different theories of formation, and the various types of guns can be successfully tried out. The greater the degree of preparedness therefore on the part of two great and ambitious nations, the more certain it is that they will some day meet in deadly combat. Piling up gunpowder is not the ideal way of preserving permanent tranquillity. Training men to shoot is not the surest method of increasing their estimate of the sacredness of human life, or of exalting in their minds the ideals of reason and conscience.

The reason why preparedness for war does not prepare for peace is because deadly weapons create an atmosphere of suspicion and fear. A gun in the hand of a child fills us with alarm, because while the child is innocent of any intention to hurt us, we do not know at what moment he might through awk-

wardness, or love of mischief, fire it off. A
man whom we do not know who persists in
standing in front of our house with a loaded
gun renders us uneasy, and he does not lessen
the disquiet within us by assuring us that he
means us no harm. If our neighbor next
door lays in, year after year, fresh stocks of
dynamite, for which we can ascertain no legitimate use, we become afraid of him even
though he is voluble in protestations of friendship. The more sweetly he talks the more
suspicious we become, provided he keeps on
increasing his stock of explosives. All the
peace talk on the part of rulers and diplomats
indulged in through the last forty years
amounted to nothing, for the reason that the
nations which spoke peace were all the time
preparing for war. Every time a statesman
declared anew the friendly feeling of his
countrymen toward the people across the
line, both countries at once ordered more guns.
The Hague Conferences said many sensible
and amiable things, but they were followed in
each case by a universal increase in armament.

When one nation prepares, its neighbors become alarmed, and when they prepare, the first nation being frightened, prepares still more thoroughly. The greater the degree of preparedness the greater of course the alarm. Military efficiency in one nation puts other nations at its mercy, and if that efficiency is pushed to the highest possible notch, there is created an almost international panic. Germany under the leadership of Prussia has since the Franco-Prussian war developed her army into a machine the most efficient known in history. The effect of that efficiency created consternation not only in France, but later on in Russia, and as soon as Germany began to add to her indomitable army a formidable fleet, then the fear seized upon Great Britain, and out of the fear of these three nations came at first the dual alliance and later the triple entente, and out of these came still later the war of ten nations. Every forward step made by Germany in military preparedness drove France and Russia and Great Britain closer together. And the closer they came together the more alarmed Germany became, and the more necessary it was that she should carry her preparedness to a still higher pitch of perfection. In spite, however, of this lesson written lurid on the sky by battle fire, there are Americans even yet blind enough to keep on saying: "Are we to be unready or ready for a possible foe? If ready, we are less likely to have the foe." Germany made for herself a ring of enemies simply by her phenomenal preparations for war, and the United States by a similar program can do the same thing.

But somebody asks, "Is not an army or a navy a police force, and can the world get on without policemen? Would you be willing to have the police force of your city disbanded and place the city at the mercy of the rowdies and toughs?" A brilliant writer has said in one of his often quoted volumes: "An army and navy are no more an incitement to war among reasonable men than a policeman is an incentive to burglary or homicide." Only a

man who is caught in the meshes of the fal-
lacious assumption that a gigantic army is a
police force, could ever write such nonsense
as that. The huge armies and navies of our
modern world are not police forces, and it is
amazing that any man capable of thinking
should imagine that they are. A police force
exists solely to maintain order. A police
force is never created either for the purpose
of aggression or defense. Policemen in one
city are not employed to resist an attack from
a neighboring city. When cities make out
their police budgets, they do not carefully
count the number of policemen in cities near
by or far away. Policemen have for their
sole function the maintenance of order. One
of their chief tasks is to direct traffic in
crowded streets, another is to give strangers
needed information, another is to help school
children across dangerous thoroughfares, another is to render assistance to those who may
be injured by a runaway horse, or run over
by an automobile. Their presence awes mischievous boys into decorum, and when a man

breaks the law it is the policeman who lays his hand upon the culprit and carries him into court. Up to a certain point an army or a navy is a police force, for up to a certain point it exists for the preservation of order. Our nation could not well get on without a small army, for there is always some sort of work which trained soldiers are best fitted to perform. Insurrections are likely to break out now and then in our great cities, and whenever they pass beyond the control of the local authorities the United States Army performs a needed service. In times of great calamity like the San Francisco fire or the Galveston tidal wave, or the Mississippi floods, there is work for soldiers to do. We shall always need soldiers as policemen, and therefore we shall always need a small army. There is work for a navy to do in years of peace. Certain kinds of national business can be best transacted by naval officers. Ships of war are needed to hold in check the rowdies of the sea, called pirates. It is for the navy to keep traffic regulations on the seas from being disregarded by vessels commanded by individuals who would, unless curbed, pay no attention to international law. There are sections of the world where law is not yet firmly established, and where the danger of popular uprisings is imminent, and so the United States must have a few gunboats which can in time of crisis be anchored in the harbors of distant cities which have for the moment fallen into the hands of a mob which might murder American citizens residing there. Nobody denies the need of a small army and a small navy, nor does anybody dispute that armies and navies have police functions which are essential to the well-ordering of the world's life. But the militarists, seizing upon this undoubted truth, exploit it in unwarranted ways, and endeavor to make it seem that an army or navy, however colossal, is nothing but a police force. Armies and navies as the world to-day knows them are only incidentally police forces. They are built for other purposes. They are for aggression and defense. They are huge machines for fighting duels. Their purpose is not to bring nations to justice but to crush nations which give offense. They are not supported to attend to traffic or to maintain order on land or sea. They are supported for the purpose of overwhelming similar aggregations of fighting strength which may be brought against them. It is a degradation of the word police to apply it to the swollen armies and navies which disgrace modern civilization. Policemen have useful work to do. Every day they render a service to the city which makes it a better place to live in. But what service can a standing army of 500,000 or a million men render to a nation commensurate with the expense of supporting it? Year after year these men give themselves solely to military drill, preparing for a war which may never come. Their life is full of monotony and tedium, their only instruments are instruments of blood, their only thoughts which lie in the line of their calling are thoughts of destruction and slaughter. Theirs is the work of aggression or defense. They are always in their imagination attacking and overwhelming some foreign nation. It is their business to conjure up foes, and to conceive plans by which these foes may be beaten. The atmosphere in which a policeman lives is not the atmosphere of the soldier. The professional soldier lives in a world in which the great word is " honor," and where patriotism is made synonymous with the sentiment " my country, right or wrong," and where a certain snobbishness and impatience are developed which express themselves in brag and ultimatums. A man who says that " an army or navy are no more an incitement to war than a policeman is an incentive to burglary or homicide " is throwing dust into the eyes of those he sets himself up to instruct. Policemen do not spend their time in scheming to overthrow other policemen, nor do they drink toasts to " the Day," nor do they write for the Sunday papers articles calling for an ever larger number of policemen. Policemen do not squander their years in drilling, nor do they live and move and have their being in the world of brute force.

I have never seen in Europe sights sadder or more tragic than the spectacle presented by her gorgeous military processions. I am always haunted by the faces of the soldiers of the armies I have seen. O the wasted years, the squandered lives, the souls that are sacrificed! When will the rulers and statesmen of Europe find pardon for the lives they have thrown away, not simply in time of war, but in the long years of armed peace! I can never enjoy a military parade, made up of men doomed to military service. The glitter of the steel, and the bright colors of the uniform, and the flash of the gold braid, and the rhythm of movement are not sufficient to blot out the blankness of the human faces, and to drive from my heart the vision of what these men might be and do if they were not being sacrificed on the altar which was raised centuries ago to a pagan god called Mars.

One of the most adroit of all the schemes adopted for the befuddling of the mind is the skillful use of the word " if." For instance,

" if an army of 200,000 Japanese should be landed some day on the coast of California, then what? " " If a German army of 100,000 should be landed to-morrow on the coast of New Jersey, what would you do? " " If a foreign nation should march through Canada to attack us, then what? " This is a form of argument which many are not able to resist. " Much virtue in if," as Touchstone declared long ago. Of all the words in the militarist vocabulary no one has greater potency than " *if.*"

But let us not forget that the pacifist also has a right to use the word " *if.*" He too can conjure up various situations which are appalling. For instance, if a comet should sweep its poisonous tail in the face of New York City, and leave its tail lying there for sixty days, what would New York do? If a meteor a hundred miles in diameter should fall on Chicago, what would become of that city? If one of the stars should break loose from its orbit and come in collision with our planet, what would happen? There is no end of the horrible possibilities which the imagination can think of, but before we are daunted by the word " if," we should look behind it, and see if it is any more than a bugaboo. If Japan should land 200,000 soldiers on the coast of California, there would be indeed serious embarrassment, at first for us, and later on for the Japanese. But why think of that before we ask the question, why should the Japanese come? Are they able to come? Have they thought of coming? Do they want to come? Have they reason for coming? Are they likely to want to come? These are the only questions with which sensible men care to deal. If the Japanese have no reason for coming, if they have laid no plans to come, if it has never entered their mind to come, then why should we, when we have so many urgent things to attend to, waste our time on a purely fanciful problem? A child can scare himself into a fit simply by imagining a ghost, but when we become men we ought to put away childish things. And as for some European nation landing on the

Atlantic seaboard and capturing New York, Philadelphia and Boston, all our chief coal fields, and all our gun factories before we know it, that is the sort of vision which a naval architect sees, and that is the kind of a dream which inventors of guns dream. There is no limit to the foolishness of the human mind when men give reins to a disordered imagination. There are at least a hundred questions which ought to be studied and answered before we take up the question as to what we could do if a foreign nation landed an immense army on our coast. We must ask how they could do it, 3000 miles from home, and why they should want to do it, and if as yet they have exhibited a disposition to do it, and what they could possibly hope to gain even if they did do it. If no nation has ever threatened to do it, or ever conceived the idea of doing it, or has any conceivable reason for wanting to do it, then why should we work ourselves into hysterics over our appalling unpreparedness? Some men say we lie at the mercy of Europe. Well, we have been lying that way for a long time, why not try it another hundred years? They say that our wealth invites attack. Why then have nations been slow in accepting the invitation? We have been wealthy a long time. They say that a foreign nation could easily take our large coast cities. Well, what would it do with them after it got them? Suppose that 200,000 soldiers land on our shore, what would they do here? They would feel very uncomfortable even at the first, and their discomfort would not grow less with time.

Look at Belgium! says a distinguished American militarist who might have made himself the peerless leader of the young men of America, and who alas, has thrown away the greatest opportunity which God has given to any American in our generation. To see a man endowed with extraordinary gifts turning his face toward the past is one of the most tragic sights which this world affords. Look at Belgium! he cries. Why should we look at Belgium? He wants us to look at it in order that we may buy more guns. Why? Because the very thing that has happened to Belgium may happen to us. To be sure, Belgium is a little country. Its area is less than 12,000 square miles, about one quarter of our Empire State, not one twentieth the size of the state of Texas. We have an area of 3,616,-000 square miles, but what happened to Belgium may just as easily happen to us! It is as likely that a nation covering three and a half million square miles shall be stepped on as it is that a nation with less than 12,000 square miles shall be so treated. Belgium has a population of less than 8,000,000, the United States has a population of one hundred million. But this makes no difference in the risk. A nation of a hundred millions is just as readily trampled on as a nation less than one twelfth of its size "Look at Belgium!" She is wedged in between a mighty empire and a great republic which are hereditary foes. When either of them wishes to strike at the other the temptation is to strike over Belgium's head. The little kingdom is so in the way that when its huge neighbors fall to fighting it is impossible for Belgium to escape. America holds the full sweep of a broad continent. God has spread his two mightiest oceans at her eastern and western doors. Instead of being crowded in between hereditary foes she stands forth isolated, independent, free. To hold up Belgium as an illustration of what is likely to come to us unless we squander additional millions on guns, is as sensible as to say: " I noticed yonder man stepped on an ant, be careful, he will next step on you."

" Look at China," the same wise man exclaims. By all means let us look at her. She has suffered many things. Rapacious and unscrupulous nations have more than once insulted her, and stolen some of her possessions. They could do this because they carried arms. But for nations to rob is disgraceful, and the disgrace is not on China but on the nations that have done her wrong. If wearing heavy armor atrophies the conscience of nations we have an additional argument against the policy of the nations which have sold themselves to Mars. Let us look at China. She is yet alive. She has lived through the storms of 4000 years. All the other nations of antiquity have gone to pieces. They all took the sword and they all perished by the sword. China the one peaceful nation alone survives. Look at China! She is proof that the nation which refuses to trust to force is unconquerable. She has been invaded, but so was Nineveh, and so were Babylon and Egypt and Greece and Persia and Rome. All military nations are sooner or later invaded, and all without exception go down at last in blood. No empire has ever gone to death except to the strains of martial music. Look at China! But some one says: "She is alive, but what does her life amount to? She has made no progress. She has contributed little to the civilization of the world. Better live like Greece and Rome, Egypt and Persia, and add something to the treasures of the world even though life be short, than live a quiescent, vegetative, ineffectual life like China, doing little to advance the progress of the race."

But China is not what she is in thought and life because of her lack of military ambition; her present condition is due to the absence of the ideals which have made Europe glorious. China for centuries was shut out from Christianity. That is the explanation of the retardation of her life. Europe owes her prestige to the mighty stimulus which was given to her by the religion of Jesus. Wherever the gospel is preached the intellect is quickened and the heart is expanded and humanity moves forward. Europe has gotten on not because of her fighting, but in spite of it. Had she never fought she would be far beyond where she now is. In spite of the loss of treasure and blood in her numberless wars, she has, because of the marvelous generosity and forgiveness of God, been able to press forward, so mighty is the force of the ideas given her by Jesus. It is not Christianity which has made Europe belligerent. Her fighting temper was an inheritance from the pagan past. She has always been cursed by the military

ideals inherited from ancient Rome. She has
for centuries been harassed and handicapped
by the military traditions which ruled the
tribes of Europe before the religion of Christ
found them. When men say: " Look at
China! That is what you come to if you disparage war, that is the doom that overtakes
you if you refuse to exalt the soldier," they
are dropping out of consideration the supreme
fact that China has for centuries been in the
grip of Confucius, while Europe has from the
fourth century been stimulated and developed
by the life giving gospel of the Son of God.

Yes, look at China, but remember the end
is not yet. You must wait to see what China
will be when she becomes Christian. All students of our modern world confess she is the
coming nation of the East. They often call
her the sleeping giant. They acknowledge
that she has in her life forces which are sure
to modify and possibly to revolutionize the
civilization of the world. What China may
yet accomplish if she opens her great heart to
Christ no man can possibly conceive. Who

knows what beautiful thing God has kept in store for her because she has never trusted to the sword. David was not allowed to build the temple in Jerusalem because his hands were stained with blood. It may be that the so-called great Christian powers will not be permitted to build the structure of the coming world because the hands of all of them are red. Who knows but what God himself may say with pride on the Judgment Day, " Look at China ! "

But must we not have an adequate navy? To be sure we must, provided we can find out what an adequate navy is. Nobody knows. Nobody can find out. The word adequate is one of the words with which the militarist works his tricks. We all know what the adjective means when we speak of an adequate definition or an adequate cause or an adequate compensation, and therefore we assume that we know what an adequate navy is. It is at that point that we fall into the militarist's clutches. He does not define the word, he simply puts it on our lips and lets it do its fatal work. What is an adequate navy? One that is sufficient, satisfactory, equal to its task. What is its task? An adequate navy, some one says, is one which would be strong enough to prevent attack, or repel invasion, or to save the nation from humiliating defeat. Now it is not possible to get a navy large enough to prevent attack. No matter how small a nation is or how poor, it will attack the mightiest empire that ever was, provided that empire does it wrong. If we ever do a nation wrong we may rest assured we shall be attacked.

Nor can we have a navy large enough to prevent invasion. We have 24,000 miles of coast line, and we cannot build ships enough to keep a foreign nation off our soil if it once determined to invade us. The navy then that is adequate must be one mighty enough to save ourselves from humiliating disaster. How large would that be? Nobody knows. One man says, it must be large enough to destroy the German navy, but another man says it must be large enough to cope with the navy

of Great Britain. Unless ours is the largest
of all the navies, we can never be master of
the seas. Of what use is it to have a second
best navy? Germany has the second best
navy to-day, yet that navy is not able to prevent German commerce from being completely
swept from off the seas. It is not able to
prevent Great Britain landing troops on
French and Belgian soil. Germany stands impotent upon the sea because her navy is only
second best. An adequate navy then for
America must be the mightiest fleet afloat. It
must outclass that of Great Britain. But even
then it would not be adequate, for Great Britain has an ally in the distant East, and that
ally helps Great Britain in her times of need.
So that to have a navy equal to the task of
insuring us against defeat, we should have to
build a navy equal to those of Great Britain
and Japan combined. And even then our
navy would be inadequate, for Great Britain
is to-day leagued with France and Russia, and
may be leagued with them again, so that to
have a navy genuinely adequate we should

234 Christianity and International Peace

have to own a navy equal to the combined
navies of the world. Men prattle about the
necessity of providing for " every possible contingency," not knowing what they say. Only
lunatics ever think of considering every possible contingency. Sensible men are content
with probabilities. It is by considering probabilities and not possibilities that we are able
to live our life. It is possible that if I walk
near the curbstone an automobile may run up
and kill me. More than once such an accident
has happened. But I cannot walk close to the
buildings for a loosened stone may fall down
and crush me. Such an accident has often
happened. If I walk in the center of the pave-
ment a mad dog may rush up and bite me.
Many a man has lost his life in that way.
If I consider possibilities I shall never go out
of the house at all. Men cannot guard themselves against every conceivable contingency.
A man may stab you in the back or side, and
therefore you must case your body in armor.
A drunken man may throw acid in your face.
You must therefore wear a helmet with a

vizor. Life becomes unendurable the moment
we set to work to provide for every eventuality.

The life of nations is equally impossible, if
you follow the life of the militarist mono-
maniacs who chatter ceaselessly about the necessity of providing for every possible contingency. Long brooding on guns and warfare has made them mad. They are victims
of distressing hallucinations. They are tortured by infernal delusions. They are willing
that a nation should use up all its income on
means of defense. They advocate policies
which lead to national bankruptcy, feeling like
many other insane men, that they are pos-
sessed of superior wisdom. How large an
army ought the United States to maintain?
One man says 125,000 and the next man
laughs at him, asserting that nothing less than
200,000 will answer. The third man is amazed
at such a paltry number, and suggests 300,000
as the minimum. A fourth man laughs loud
at such niggardly conservatism, and declares
that half a million men are none too many.

The next man, still better posted in regard to
our national needs, assures us that a million
men would be quite moderate, considering our
size and wealth and danger. If I were a militarist I should say two million at the lowest,
and that three million would be better. It is
only when you get into the millions that you
approach the size of the great armies of Europe. Why have an army at all, unless you
have the largest and best? There has never
yet been on any land an army which the military experts counted adequate, and there has
never been on any sea a fleet which the naval
experts of the nation possessing it considered
sufficient. The only definition of an adequate
navy or army which it is possible to write is
— It is an army or navy larger than the one
which we already have. When the militarist
asks you to subscribe to his doctrine of an
" adequate " army or navy, he is simply asking you to favor an increase in the army and
naval budgets.

Somebody says, we must have an army and

navy simply for defense. " Not one cent for aggression, but as many millions as necessary for defense," was the ejaculation the other day of an enthusiastic patriot in the East. All such talk is stupid. There are no aggressive navies or armies on the earth. They are all defensive. It was expressly understood by the Parliaments which organized and built the armies and navies of modern Europe that they were solely for defense. Germany has built up an army to defend herself, and Great Britain has led the world in dreadnoughts in order to ward off attack. Not a cent has been wasted by any European nation for purposes of aggression. Every nation meekly takes up the duty of providing for its defense. And so this is a defensive war. All the nations are fighting in defense. Not one is responsible for the war. No one wanted it. No one has designs of aggression. Every nation is fighting for the defense of its own hearthstones and fields. If, therefore, we launch dreadnoughts for defense, other nations will also launch other dreadnoughts for defense, and thus the wasting and demoralizing game will go on. The man who talks about defense with the notion that by the use of that word he can get the world on, is a man whom experience can teach nothing. We might as well say distinctly at the launching of each new American battleship: "This is for aggression." The effect on other nations would be the same as though we said: "This is merely for defense." The ostrich hides his little head in the sand and thinks his body is invisible. The militarized and duped American thinks he can favor a navy for defense, and escape the curse by which Europe has been overwhelmed.

But some one asks, If France had not spent millions on her armies and guns and forts, where would she have been when the German army started for Paris? The answer is that if it had not been for the French military bustle and the loaning of French millions to Russia for the purchase of additional guns, the German army might never have started toward

Paris. When men say where would Great Britain be to-day if she had not built up the greatest navy in the world? the answer is she might not be in a great war. If she had not insisted on the right to dominate all the seas, and had not sung so loud and so exultingly " Britannia rule the wave," and if she had not claimed the right of seizure of private property on the sea in time of war, then the whole history of Europe might have been different. So long as Great Britain holds her present policy she has got to have her navy, but her policy must be changed before there can be permanent peace in the world. So long as all the nations of Europe have their barbaric policies of statesmanship, just so long must they trust to bayonets and shells for protection when the storm which they have created bursts upon them.

Some one says, " If the other nations of Europe arm themselves from crown to toe, then we must arm ourselves too. There can be no reduction in armaments until all agree to act together. One nation cannot run the risk of being trampled on by its armed neighbors. Our policy must be determined solely by the policy of Europe." If this be so, then it behooves us to throw the entire weight of our republic into the movement for the formation of a League of Peace. Universal reduction in armament should be our cry day and night. It should ring out loud and clear so that the nations of the whole earth can hear it. Our President should shout it and every member of his cabinet, and every member of Congress, and every preacher and every editor, and every college president, and every college professor, and every college student, and every other man of influence in the whole land should demand that the hour for reduction of armaments has come. It is not for us at this time to be talking about more powder and guns. Our business is to give our entire thought to the great problem of bringing the nations into an agreement to lay down their arms. But suppose Europe will not listen? What if she turns a deaf ear, and goes on after the war ends in her old policy of armed peace, then what should our policy be? It is at this point that the wisest of good men disagree. For myself, I would say: "Let America go alone. Let her set an example. Let her exhibit a courage and a faith worthy of a Christian nation." If you say, "Ah, that would be a great risk," I admit it, but I hold it would not be so great a risk as we run in building up a greater army and a greater navy. When so many nations have taken the risks of war, would it not be worth while for one nation to take the risks of peace? Who knows what might happen if a great republic like ours should take a magnificent risk for God?

VI

What, then, Shall We Do?

WE come to the end of our journey. We must now face the question to which the course of our thought has led us. What shall we do? The world being what it is, what are we going to do about it? In a situation such as the one in which our generation finds itself, what can one do? "The end of life," says Carlyle, "is not a thought, but an action." The end of a course of lectures is not a thought, or a feeling, or an aspiration, but a course of conduct. My work is not done until I attempt to answer this question: What shall we do? It is not enough to describe a dilemma. There must be a suggestion as to how to deal with it. It will never do to diagnose a disease, and go off without prescribing a remedy. To condemn an evil is futile unless a way of deliverance is pointed out. He who helps us most is not the man who can picture most graphically past blunders or present distresses, but who can indicate the path along which our feet may travel toward better and brighter days.

The first feeling which seizes one on contemplating the international situation is one of helplessness. What can I do? The answer is obviously, nothing. We sink back exhausted by the thought of our own impotency. What can any one man or woman do to change the temper or the habit of the world? What can a score of men or a hundred or a thousand or ten thousand do? The heart loses hope the moment we ask the question, "What shall we do? What can anybody do?" Have not good people been trying for centuries to make war impossible, and what have they accomplished? Have we not Peace Societies, and Peace Foundations, and Church Peace Unions, and International Peace Bureaus, and Women's Peace Federations, and multitudinous agencies for the overthrow of the war traders and the war makers, but what have they been able to accomplish? If all these have proved insufficient to meet the situation, what then can we do?

Many of us do nothing but cultivate emotions. We feel and we feel intensely. We feel bad. We feel mad. We blaze with indignation. We groan. We cry out in pain. But that is all. Our feeling simply wears us out. It does not accomplish anything. It makes no impression on the policy of government. It does not change the current of the life of the world.

Others of us both feel and speak. We break into articulate expression. We exclaim. We declaim. We criticise. We find fault. We indulge in good round full toned denunciation. But what do we accomplish? Congress does not hear us. Those who sit in high places do not heed us. The world remains what it was. Some of us are prolific in good wishes. We overflow with them. We wish we could stop the war. Of course we cannot. We wish men had more sense.

They have not. We wish we were President of the United States. We are not, and are not likely to be. We wish we could run the world for a little while, but God is not willing to trust us. And thus we smother ourselves with our wishes.

There is no end of good wishes. But it must be confessed that good wishes are not sufficient to redeem a world. Something tougher and more dynamic than wishes is essential to keep the world on the path that leads to life. The horrors of war have been frequently painted by orators and artists, its brutalities and savageries have been set forth by essayists and historians for many a hundred years. Of its unspeakable horribleness there can now remain not a vestige of doubt, for the present war with a brush of fire has written its atrocities across the sky. Only an imbecile can go on now prating about the glory of war. But shuddering over the terrors of war is not sufficient to deliver us from the grip of it. We may say with unction that war is hell, but saying that does not put out the flames of it. That is the weakness of too much of our speaking and writing; it is vivid in adjectives, but is not rich in creative thought. Reformers tell us the predicament into which we have fallen, but they forget to tell us how to get out. They tear to tatters verbally the evil which they lament, but they give no directions as to how the evil is to be abolished.

Let us now turn to the practical question: What can we do as American citizens toward the solution of this greatest of world problems? It is evident that we cannot as individuals do anything directly to bring pressure to bear upon European policy. No one of us, or any thousand of us, can by word or deed modify the program of any government beyond the sea. Whatever we do we must do through our own government, and what we do through our government must be done through the people whom we are able to reach. In the long run our officials represent the sentiment and ideals of the voters. We cannot get our National Congress far in advance of the average sentiment of the country. Our national policy will on the whole reflect quite accurately the thought and feeling of the masses of our people.

Here then is the place to begin. We must start with the people, with that particular group of people who happen to be nearest to us, and who can be in any way influenced by us. Every man has influence, and can make a mark of some sort on the minds and lives of the people around him. Public opinion is the real ruler of this country. To-morrow it is going to be the ruler of the world. It is higher than Congresses and Parliaments, more potent than Emperors and Kings. This world belongs to the people, and soon or late they are going to rule it. Now public opinion is formed by those men and women who have ideas and who dare to express them. Ideas are impotent unless they are expressed. As soon as they are expressed they drop into human minds and at once begin their work. They are seeds and like seeds they sprout and grow. No one can tell what a harvest will ultimately come from the planting of an idea.

One reason why the practice of war has continued to the present hour is because the idea of war has been made glorious to the imagination. War has been extolled by philosophers and political leaders as a school of the virtues, a developer of that which is finest and strongest in a nation's life. It is in war, wise men have repeatedly said, that a man has the finest opportunity to show the greatness of his soul. It is only by war that nations are saved from inertia and sloth and moral decay. This is the idea that has been set forth by historians, and spread on the canvas by artists, and embodied in song by poets, and glorified by orators in their loftiest flights. Young men in all countries have been trained to think of patriotism and a gun as belonging together, and to die for one's country on the battlefield has been counted the supreme manifestation of human nobility. In every land, war has been decked out with lustrous robes, and the soldier has been placed upon a pedestal denied to the civilian. For long centuries the statues were largely those of the war makers, and the most interesting of the biographies were those of men who had won renown upon the battlefield.

It is not easy to take down an ancient ideal and substitute another in its place. To do this is the work of years. It is a work of education, and the work must be carried on in all schools throughout the country from the lowest to the highest. Not only must there be changes in the text books, but there must be changes in the viewpoint of many of the teachers. Many teachers, especially in our colleges, are wedded to pagan ideals. They are blind to spiritual realities. They possess technical knowledge within narrow circles, but they do not know how to interpret the signs of the times. It must be shown by men capable of doing it, that war is not the only school of patriotism, or the supreme school of virtue. The hallucination that war is essential to national or individual development must be overthrown by men who see facts as they are. Struggle is indeed necessary for human development, but the struggle of war is only one form of struggle, and it is a form whose usefulness has long since been outgrown. The struggles of the future are to be in the realm of the spirit. Men will always be called upon to grapple with difficulties, and to face opposition, but the struggle wrought out by bayonets belongs to an age left behind. The moral fiber of men will never rot, provided they have high ideals and a determination to attain them. The heroism displayed in war is not so splendid as that which is nurtured in peace. There is in peace the call for continuous courage, whereas in war there are only a few moments when a man is called to exhibit courage of a lofty type. In peace there is no excitement, no tumult of the blood, often no heartening sympathy of comrades to urge men forward, whereas in battle men are carried on by the mass of numbers and the wild fury of the hour. It must be shown that to save men is a higher form of service than to kill them, and that it calls for the exercise of a larger number of the highest faculties of the soul. To lift a city to a higher level of thought and action is a more difficult piece of work and demands a finer heroism than to level it by means of howitzers. To cast the evil spirits out of a city, is a more hazardous undertaking than to pour upon it explosives from the sky. The work of dropping bombs on women and children is a bit of savagery, not at all different from the hellish cruelty of the Indians who in their raids scalped women and children as well as men. There will come a time when all the arts of modern warfare will be held in universal detestation. To blow men to atoms at a distance of five miles is not heroic. To drive old men and women and invalids into the fields to starve is not chivalric. To raze to the ground the homes of peasants, and send them out into the winter storms is not an exhibition of nobility. The men who do these things will not stand on pedestals in that better time toward which the world's face is set.

It must be made clear to all American youth that the dangers of the Republic are not with-

out, but within. Our deadliest foes are not
beyond the sea, but within our own cities.
The enemies which we have most to fear are
ignorance, and greed, and drunkenness, and
lust, and cruelty, and irreverence, and dis-
honesty, and lawlessness, and wild blasts of
ungovernable mob-passion. Against these,
siege guns are no protection, nor can they be
guarded against by fleets in the sky. We
must root out the notion that a nation is defended by battleships or battalions, and must
make it clear that a nation's safest and last
defenses are the spirit and character of its
people.

Man is by nature a fighting animal. The
military instincts are planted in him. He is
built for the express purpose of fighting his
way. All real life is warfare, and man's belligerent instincts must be trained to fight the
battles of the Lord. To the end of time men
must continue to be good soldiers, but the
weapons of their warfare will not be carnal.
There are swords sharper than steel, and there
are forces more efficient than the mightiest of

the explosives. A Harvard professor wrote a suggestive essay once on " Moral equivalents for war." The best of all equivalents is a faithful Christian life. The supreme school of virtue is the school of the Son of God. It is the academy of patriotism. It is the university of courage.

The time has come when we must make war upon war with a boldness of attack and a tenacity of purpose which has never heretofore been displayed. They are in error who imagine that Christian virtue is passive. The non-resistance which the New Testament inculcates does not lie down and do nothing. It is the most vigorous and daring of all forms of aggression. Jesus resisted evil at all points and with all his might. He said: " I must go to Jerusalem." Why? Because in Jerusalem the foes were the mightiest and it was there that the fiercest of all the battles had to be fought. He had to go to the capital, and that is where we must go. He went there to drive out the miscreants who were defiling the national life at its fountain, and it is in Wash-

ington City that we must meet and overthrow
the men who are squandering the wealth and
jeopardizing the stability of the American Republic.

The European War was made inevitable by
the foolish thinking and exasperating action
of a few classes of men.   The masses of Europe are amiable and peace-loving people.
The Slav does not thirst for the blood of the
Teuton, nor does the Teuton long to slaughter
the Slav.   The German does not aspire to slay
the Englishman, nor does the Englishman
nourish the ambition to crush the German.
The war was made inevitable by the long continued scheming and plotting of industrious
companies of mischief makers.   It is not difficult to see just who they were, and every class
of mischief maker in Europe is represented in
our own country.   If allowed to carry out
their plans, they will bring us to the same
abyss into which Europe has fallen.   Let us
take a square look at these makers of trouble.

First of all, we must deal with our military and naval officers — not all of them, but

with those who set themselves up as instructors of the nation and dictators of national policy. There are men in the United States army and navy who need to be reminded that they are officers of the government, and that it is not becoming in them to carry on a ceaseless propaganda for the aggrandizement of the military and naval establishments. Some of these men are incessantly talking, and others are everlastingly writing. They draw large salaries from the government for one form of duty, and then devote their time to business for which they are not employed. The loquacity of a few of them is exasperating. They are always whispering to reporters, giving them inside information in regard to the unpreparedness of the country, others are prominent at public banquets at which they never fail to sound a note of alarm. In every hour of national excitement the voices of certain Commodores and Colonels are heard throughout the land. Those who are not expert in speech, make themselves felt through their pen. They write for the

magazines and Sunday papers, and the burden
of their story is always the need of more guns.
Some of the ablest of them write volumes
which obtain a wide circulation, and the ideas
which they sow are ideas which will some day
bring forth harvests of death. They glorify
the gospel of force. They exalt military
ideals. They stir ambitions in men's hearts
which menace the welfare of the world. Only
recently there died an officer of the United
States navy who for years had been an indefatigable teacher of the gospel of force, gath-
ering at his feet not only thousands of young
men of our own country but tens of thousands
in countries beyond the sea. That man was
one of the forces which helped to bring on the
present war. He wrote the book which perhaps more than any other book fired the Kaiser
to build up a colossal German navy. It is said
by a friend of his that the present war daunted
him, and that in his last hours the foundations of his life-long teaching were shaken.
It is a practical question which we might as
well face now as later, is it wise for the United

States government to allow the officers of our army and navy to hold interviews with reporters, to talk about our military and naval policies at banquets, and to write books dealing with questions of international politics, and exploiting the gospel of military preparedness and efficiency? We have never had a subsidized church, or press, or theater, and it is time to ask ourselves if we are to have a body of subsidized writers and speakers who shall make it their chief business to keep the nation in a state of chronic alarm over the deficiencies of our military and naval equipment, and to poison with false ideals the minds of the youth of the land. It is one of the serious perils of armed peace, that it gives a large company of able and virile men abundant leisure for the propagation of the views which are dear to their hearts. Germany has for forty years been faithfully instructed by a corps of able army and naval officers in the philosophy of militarism, and there are officers in our army and navy who are completely captivated by the German ideal.

Moreover, these officers are permitted, in large numbers, to make their home in Washington City. Living there, it is wellnigh impossible for them to keep their hands off of Congress. They get acquainted with the congressmen and senators, and by various arts of persuasion win these men to favor their plans. Justice Brewer of the United States Supreme Court spent the leisure hours of the closing years of his illustrious life in warning his countrymen against the growing power of the army and navy in the National Capital. In one of his addresses he called attention to the fact that at that time there were 727 officers of army and navy, active and retired, residing in Washington City, besides the families of many officers deceased. Now all these officers have their relatives and friends, some of them men of high position and great influence, and when the officers combine their forces with those of their friends and families they exert an influence on national legislation which carries with it incalculable dangers. There is already at Washington a military-naval oligarchy which will, unless checked, prove to be the most dangerous oligarchy which our government has ever been obliged to cope with. I once asked a congressman why Congress persisted in squandering the people's money on battleships and cruisers, and his reply was: " You have no idea of the tremendous power exerted on Congress by army and naval officers and their friends."

In this work of influencing Congress the Navy League plays an ever increasing part. By its agents, official and volunteer, in various parts of the country, it is able to stir up periodic excitement over national unpreparedness, and when the time arrives for voting on the national budget, a heavy shower of letters usually falls on the congressional desks.   The threatening international weather which occurs every year at the time when the army and naval estimates for the coming year are determined, is surmised by many to have some occult relation to the Navy League.   It was the Navy Leagues of Europe which helped create the situation of which the war of ten nations came. Army and Navy Leagues cannot fail to be a pest and menace in every country in which they gain a footing. Men who love their country and mankind should resolutely hold aloof from such organizations. No matter what illustrious names may be flaunted on their banners, they are mischief makers, and are especially dangerous in a Republic.

It is because of their intrusion in politics, and their disposition to attempt to mould the policy of the nation that an increase in the number of military and naval officers should be looked upon with concern. To add, for instance, a thousand new officers to the United States army, seems on the face of it a very small matter. But it must be borne in mind that every new officer is a possible propagandist and politician, that he has brothers or uncles or friends whose active support for new military schemes he can secure, and that soon or late, we may find him comfortably settled in Washington City, quietly enjoying the comfort of armed peace, and drawing a salary for writing articles and books on the supreme importance of a nation spending most of its income on guns.

This is the direction in which it is not wise for a Republic to go. History shows that even monarchies find it difficult to cope with their own military forces after such forces reach a certain growth. The army becomes a disturbing factor in the national life, the hotbed of feverish ambitions and insurrectionary movements. More than one king has been ousted from his throne by the very army which was created to defend him. But republics have less resisting power to military encroachments than monarchies have. In republics there is a constant change of officials. The term of office is at longest but a few years. One administration follows another, and men who were in the seats of power but yesterday are to-day so poor that there is no one to do them reverence. If, now, you establish in the National Capital a caste of army and naval officials whose term of service is of necessity continuous and extended, you have a body of men whose power for working their will, runs far beyond that of any other class. Just a few shrewd and far sighted and determined men, secure in office for a generation, can so manipulate the various political factions and parties as to work out in time the fulfillment of their schemes. By pitting party against party, and taking advantage of every opportunity which the shifting tides of party prosperity offer, they finally get the better of their antagonists, and carry their cause to triumph. Republics and military oligarchies have never been able to live long together. Soon or late the strong man on horseback appears and the civil power goes down. It seems absurd to us to-day to imagine that our army and navy should ever overturn our republic. It would indeed be absurd to say that they could do it now. But who knows what may be possible in the course of years if a policy of continuous military expansion is adopted, and military and naval leaders are allowed an ever increasing place in the domain of national legislation. The militarists got such a grip on Germany and have carried their measures in such a high handed manner there, that one-third of all the German people have been driven into Socialism. Great Britain has for generations kept down the size of her army, but last year she discovered to her amazement when Parliament was considering a certain policy to be pursued in Ireland, that high officers in the British army were not afraid to say that they would not carry out the Government's will. In other words, the British army, in the person of various notable officials, lifted itself above the civil power, plainly saying that Great Britain ought to be ruled by the army, and not by representatives chosen by the people in Parliament assembled. If these things can happen beyond the sea, why should they not happen here, not in the green tree but in the dry? National calamities do not come in the twinkling of an eye, not even in this generation or the next. They come as the result of a gradual yielding to false ideals carried on through a long succession of years. Our old-fashioned American fear of standing armies is a fear that should never be permitted to die out. It was created in the hearts of our ancestors by the bitter tribulations through which they had passed, and a careful reading of history is sufficient to prove that for republics militarism is a swift and inevitable road to death.

Next to the military and naval experts who have accepted the ideals of Bernhardi, in their power to work mischief stand the men who make fortunes by trading in the munitions of war. Commercialism was one of the forces which hurled Europe to destruction. The gun makers and the ship builders and the explosive manufacturers have helped to deluge Europe in blood. No men in our generation have been more alert, industrious, and masterful than they. By employing brilliant designers and inventors, they have been able to get out each year a superior class of goods, which it has been deemed necessary for the nations to purchase, lest one of them fall behind the other. Big guns have been followed by guns still bigger, and these by guns bigger still. One ship

has led to the creation of another type of
ship, and this has necessitated still another,
until every nation possesses a long list of various kinds of fighting vessels, and the list
is not yet completed. When the armor of the
dreadnought was made so thick that it was impossible to pierce it, it became necessary to
invent a torpedo; but having the torpedo, it
was necessary to have a boat which could fire
it, and thus there came into existence the torpedo boat. This being exceedingly dangerous,
it was necessary to invent a boat to destroy
it, and thus there was added to the fleet the
torpedo boat destroyer. This being an exceedingly dangerous vessel, it was necessary
to come at it, if possible, from below the water, and so the submarine was invented, with
a lot of complicated apparatus the like of
which had never been known before. And
thus the game of invention has gone merrily
on, the scientists and architects reveling in
their ingenuity, the ship builders enlarging
their plants, the governments meekly paying
the bills. And what bills! The nations

loaded themselves in times of peace with debts that it will take generations to pay. This wild extravagance was counted necessary, however, because if you are in a military or naval race, nothing short of the newest and most expensive weapon is adequate. And so in all the great Christian countries powerful firms of ship builders and gun makers have been making enormous fortunes. Their cupidity has grown by what it has fed on, and every year their zeal has become hotter and their policies more aggressive and unscrupulous. The full story of the workings of these corporations has not yet been written. Enough has been found out to make it clear that militarism on its commercial side is one of the rottenest things under heaven. These firms have in certain cases been found out to be engaged in the diabolical work of fomenting international suspicions, and of launching war panics. When nations grow lukewarm in buying guns, they must be frightened into it. Vested interests must pay rich dividends. Costly machinery must be kept at work. It

will never do to have men idle in the great
shipyards or armor-plate mills or gun factories, and so, year after year, the world has
been over-run by a pack of agents and pro-
moters whose supreme business has been to
create a larger market for explosives and
armor plate and guns. Where the carcass is,
there do the vultures gather. Where the appropriations are immensest there you find a
throng eager to get a share. The private manufacture of the munitions of war should not
be tolerated. Private gain by the manufacture
of the implements of destruction, that is a
temptation which must be swept out of reach.
Whatever guns and ships are needed must be
made by the government. No private corpo-
ration should be permitted to coin gold by
catering to the military and naval establishments. Syndicates must not be allowed to
work in collusion with one another — as they
have long done in this country — sending in
identical bids, taking the government by the
throat and saying: " This is the price which
we demand, and there is nothing for you to

do but to pay it." When we shall have swept
the armor plate and ship building and gun
lobbyists out of the national halls of legislation, we shall have taken an important step in
the suppression of war panics, and in cutting
down the dimensions of military and naval
budgets. The traffic of the war traders is
the greatest swindle perpetrated on the world
since Tetzel sold indulgences.

What makes the military experts and the
traders doubly dangerous is because they have
as their coadjutors able representatives of the
unscrupulous section of the daily press. When
the proprietor of a newspaper is a jingoist
and a conscienceless fomenter of strife, it is
hard to set limits to the mischief he is able to
accomplish. There are men so low down in
the scale of moral development that they deliberately fan the flames of international suspicion and hatred. They hire men to write
insulting editorials about foreign nations.
They admit into their columns letters from
persons as depraved as themselves. They take
delight in jabbing other nations. They gloat

over the foibles and follies of other peoples.
In times of international tension, these men
invariably say the exasperating word. They
poison the wells of international good will.
They impugn the motives of foreign statesmen. They put the worst possible construc-
tion on every act of a foreign power. They
reprint articles from other papers inspired by
the same spirit of Gehenna. To fill up the
measure of their guilt, they publish fake interviews, and narrate things that never happened.
They sometimes make corrections two days
later, but it is then too late. The poison has
been injected, and is already doing its fatal
work. No one can understand the great European War without taking into account the
journalists of Europe. In every European
capital there have been for a generation a
group of mischief making writers, and not until you have examined the files of the leading
newspapers in Berlin and Paris, Petrograd
and Vienna and London for the last dozen
years can you fully understand why the greatest calamity of all history has fallen. Men by

their pens can set a continent on fire. Many of the wisest and noblest men of our modern world are editors. Some of the worst men are editors also. When some future Dante paints his picture of Inferno, he will thrust into the lowest round a company of reptilian creatures, who were given the opportunity of lifting the world into new faith and hope and love by the printing press which God entrusted to their keeping, but who used it only to set nations against one another, and to drench a continent with blood. Some of the vilest of all the newspaper proprietors of the world are found in our own country, and we must do all we can to break their power. The men who write against foreign nations are always the men who favor a bigger army and an always growing navy. You can count upon them always giving wrong advice in an hour of crisis, of urging the government into courses it should avoid.

The pestiferous newspaper proprietor is one of the most difficult of all mischief makers to deal with. We cannot take him out and

shoot him because he shrieks for war. Even
when war comes, there is no law by which
we can place him in the first line of battle,
although that is where he ought to be. We
cannot have a national censor. We are living
in a country of free thought and free speech.
Free speech carries with it a free press. As
a people we could never submit to constant
governmental interference with our papers.
Editors like other men must be free. To publish foolishness, if they are so disposed, is a
privilege which we cannot by statutory enact-
ment take away from them. What then can
be done? There is nothing to do but to render the people immune to their poison. If
you can make the masses of the people sensible,
then fools in newspaper offices can do no
damage. If we can create a feeling of good
will in the hearts of our people, then the
flaming tirades of the newspaper jingoist will
not set the land on fire. You must have com-
bustibles as well as a match to create a conflagration. The newspaper man has a match.
We cannot take it from him, but his match

will never burn us up, if in the heart of the
nation there is nothing which will catch fire
from the brimstone which he scatters. Newspaper men are peculiarly sensitive to popular
opinion. They scrutinize with searching eye
the figures on the ledger in the counting room.
We have in America probably as good a press
as we deserve. When our national character
improves, our papers will be better. There is
no way of keeping injurious microbes out of
your body. The only salvation lies in taking
in so many good microbes that they will neu-
tralize the poisonous effect of the bad. We
cannot eliminate all foolish and hot headed
editors from the country, but we can increase
every year the number of sane editors until at
last the dunces can do no harm. When you see
in your newspaper a malicious article written
with the evident intent of stirring up feeling
hostile to a foreign nation, why not write a
note of protest, not for publication, but to let
the editor know that you do not like what he
is doing? He may care nothing for you, but
if a hundred persons wrote to him, all uttering

a similar protest, he would begin to think; and if five hundred wrote he would probably say: "This evidently is not what the people want." Definite Christian opinion continuously expressed, not to men who have nothing to do with the papers, but to the editors themselves, is the agency which, under God, is going in time to cleanse and redeem even the worst specimens of our American daily press.

And this is the way in which we must deal with the mischief makers who succeed in getting into Congress. We have always since the foundation of our government had at least one fool in Congress, and most of the time we have had two. Occasionally we have had even more. Now this is a misfortune that cannot easily be remedied. If you have democracy at all, you must take with it the risks and the limitations of democracy. When you let all sorts and conditions of men vote, you are certain to elect all sorts and conditions of men to serve you in the halls of legislation. The demagogue will be able to

slip now and then into Congress, and so will
the jingoist, and so will the monomaniac who
plays all his music on one string. But this
need not disturb us. Let us work still more
assiduously to create a sane and wholesome
public opinion, for Congress is sensitive to
what people are thinking and saying, and the
mass of congressmen are certain to be
swayed and directed by the sentiment that is
hottest and strongest in the public mind. The
jingoist military expert, and war trader, and
newspaper proprietor, and congressman are all
harmless and impotent, if only the masses of
our people are enemies of militarism and
steadfast devotees of justice and peace.

But we must go further than this. It is
not enough to criticise foolish talking and
writing. We must create ways of holding
the evil propensities of humanity in check.
We must organize the moral forces of the
world. There is no doubt more peace sentiment than war sentiment in the world, but
militarism organizes the war sentiment, and
the peace sentiment is allowed to run to waste.

Had the peace sentiment of Europe been mobilized with half the efficiency with which the forces of destruction were mobilized, there never would have been this war. Pacifists are simply puppets in the hands of the militarists because the latter know the value of organization and concentrate their power on the positions which must be attacked and taken. They create institutions to embody their ideals, and to make them effective in the life of nations. Not until the peace lovers of the world focus their eyes on a few definite things which must be accomplished, can we hope to bring the world into a state of permanent international peace.

First of all, we Americans ought to work for the establishment of a new department of our government, a department whose special and exclusive business shall be cultivating and maintaining international good will. If we have a Secretary of War, why not have a Secretary of Peace? If we appropriate a hundred million dollars for our army, and a hundred and fifty million dollars for our navy, can we not afford to appropriate, say, ten million dollars annually for a department of peace? Are we to go on forever assuming that battleships and fortifications and bayonets are our only lines of defense? We all know that there are defenses spiritual as well as physical. I can defend myself from a man by a club, but I can also defend myself from him by a friendship. The second is easier, more sensible, and safer. A man who depends on a club is never altogether sure of his defense. The club may break, or he may not swing it quickly enough, or it may not land on the right spot, but a friendship if genuine can always be relied on. Why should not nations set themselves seriously to the task of making friends of all their neighbors? Why should not money and time be expended in the work of drawing them together? At present we have a set of salaried officials who are constantly on the lookout for evidences of evil intentions in our neighbors. They brood over problematic perils. They plan for wars which are yet to come. Why not have an-

other set of national officials who shall give
all their time to the cultivation of feelings of
confidence and good will, who shall look for
every slightest manifestation of friendliness,
and who shall publish from time to time in
official documents the appreciative things
which are said about us in foreign lands?
When we returned a part of the Boxer in-
demnity, we built a powerful fortification
against China. That single act of generosity
was worth more to us in the way of defense
than the launching of a dozen dreadnoughts.
When newspapers begin to publish alarming
news items on the hostility of Japan, the government should be prepared to send a hundred of our most distinguished and fair
minded citizens to confer with representatives
of the Japanese people, and bring back a re-
port of facts as they are. The Americans
who fear Japan are prolific in plans to guard
ourselves against her, but their plans are fear-
fully expensive, and it is not certain how
successfully they would work. But all that is
needed to keep Japan and the United States

friends forever is courtesy and brotherliness and the full toned trust of all our people. Japan is a little nation, struggling amid many difficulties to a larger measure of the light which has fallen on our western world. She has no desire for any of our territory. She has no wish or thought of fighting us. All she craves is simply friendly coöperation with us in working out the great world problems. A Secretary of Peace could counteract the disturbing influences of mischief makers on both sides of the Pacific.

There are those who are always looking with dark misgivings upon the attitude of European nations. Some are afraid of Russia, others of Germany, and others of Great Britain. Our only defense, they say, is a powerful navy, powerful enough to meet any possible eventuality. To protect ourselves they are willing to curtail every other item of national expenditure, to postpone the carrying out of every scheme of social betterment, sacrificing all internal improvements to the building up of a fleet which shall dominate the seas. But why not try a better way? Bulwarks made of steel are extravagantly expensive, and moreover they may fail us in the crucial hour. Instead of building new battleships just now, why not save our money and at the end of the war go among the European nations doing good? When the war is over, why not, instead of launching new dreadnoughts, try to bind up some of Europe's wounds? Instead of spending thirty million dollars on two new dreadnoughts, why not give it as a present to the European nations most impoverished by the war, for the purpose of erecting and endowing in each one of them an orphan asylum for the education of the boys and girls whose fathers died on the battlefield? Dreadnoughts are provocative of ugly feelings. We may call them defensive dreadnoughts, but they are offensive to all the nations which look into the bore of their guns. Institutions built by our money for the help of the helpless in foreign lands would plead like angels for us, and hold back statesmen, even disposed to insolence and aggression, from perpetrating

upon us an act of discourtesy or injustice.
There is nothing so mighty in this world as
simple kindness. Thrice is he armed who has
a heart so true and gentle that it calls out
from others feelings of respect and love. Let
the United States open a new chapter in the
world's history by seating in its cabinet a
minister, entrusted with the work of further-
ing International Peace.

But we cannot work alone. The world's
problems demand many co-laborers. We must
join with others in the creation of new institutions for the safeguarding of the interests
of the nations. The two Conferences at The
Hague were prophetic. They were valuable
not so much for what they accomplished as
for pointing out the direction in which the
world must move. Provision must now be
made for their automatic periodic meeting.
Such a conference must meet not because
some ruler sees fit to call it, but because the
year has arrived when, according to the constitution, it is time for the world's counsellors
again to assemble. There must be an In-

ternational Court. It must be permanent.
Its Judges must be ready at all times to ad-
judicate the matters presented to them. This
court must be backed up by an international
police force. To this force, each nation must
contribute its quota of fighting ships. Re-
calcitrant and lawless nations must be given
to know that they cannot do as they please.
Treaties are not scraps of paper, but sacred
obligations to be solemnly kept. If a nation
is not willing to keep them, she must be
coerced into obedience by her right-minded
neighbors. In short, the world must be organized. The nations must be federated.
The whole planet must be brought under
law. No one or two nations must ever
again be permitted to hurl civilization into a
ditch.

The only objection to this scheme is its
difficulty. It will take a long time to bring
it about. Everybody can see that it is difficult,
and those who have studied it longest are
most aware how baffling the difficulties are.
But because a thing is difficult is no reason

for giving it up. If the world cannot well
get on without a world government, then a
world government we must have. It must
be devised and carved out by men. That is
what men are for. They are given the
privilege of living in order that they may provide the things which life needs. It was a
difficult thing to bring our thirteen colonies
together Many men said offhand that it
could not be done. Some who at first
thought it possible, gave up hope after the
first few struggles. But there were enough
men of faith and courage to carry the enterprise through. To their lasting renown they
persevered. To the eternal welfare of mankind they succeeded. The fact that it was so
tremendously difficult increases our gratitude
to the heroes who achieved it. That is the
best thing which the new world has ever yet
done. Nothing else is comparable with it.
To devise a form of government under which
it is possible for forty-eight commonwealths
to live together in harmony is one of the half
dozen greatest triumphs of human genius.

Nothing superior to it has ever been attempted or accomplished. Only one thing more difficult can be conceived of, and that is the organization of countries under different flags into a world federal union. The United States of the World, this is the solution of the war problem. The difficulties are vast, but they are not unconquerable. The obstacles are numberless, but they are not insuperable. The disappointments and delays will be vexatious, but they need not be overwhelming. God will give us time, and we shall ultimately accomplish what God intends shall be done. Why should any American wince in the presence of such a problem? If Washington and Franklin and Jefferson and Hamilton and Adams had courage sufficient to launch a new experiment upon the world, and trust to the storms of the future, a government built on the principle that all men are created equal, and that life and liberty and the pursuit of happiness are to be counted natural and inalienable rights, shame on us if we slink away from this still larger problem of organizing the nations into a world wide commonwealth! To be as good as our fathers — as Wendell Phillips used to say — we must be better than they. We are not worthy of our lineage if we dare not attempt larger things than have ever before been attempted. Faith and courage then are what our Republic just now most needs. We are face to face with a world crisis. We have an opportunity granted to no other nation. We can blaze a new track through the forest. We can turn the stream of history into a new channel. We have come to the parting of the roads. We can follow the wasting precedents of the past, or we can attempt a beautiful and original thing. We can say boldly to all the nations of the earth: "Let us begin to reduce our military and naval equipment; let us disband some of our regiments, and cut down our naval appropriations, and spend more of our money hereafter for the welfare of the people." We can say: "We cannot do this alone, but we are willing to lead the way. We are willing to go first, and we are willing to go farthest. We are glad to set you an example. We are willing to replace the arbitrament of force by the arbitrament of reason. We are ready to submit every international dispute to arbitration." O that our government might say that, and that all the people might say Amen. The government cannot say it unless the people want it. Ours is a government of the people and by the people and for the people, and the government cannot run beyond the ideals of the people. A government that leaps beyond the moral attainments of the people is a government which is doomed to humiliation. What the government says is of slight worth unless it expresses what is immovably fixed in the minds and hearts of the people.

And so we come at last to the most indispensable work of all, that is the spiritual rebirth of our nation. There is no solution for any of our problems except through repentance and prayer. There is no possibility of our going into the kingdom of peace unless we are born again. The world problem as

well as the city problem and the individual
problem is a religious problem. Its solution
is found in the realm of the spirit. A leader
of distinction has recently said that religion
offers us no hope of a way to international
peace, but that we are to find redemption in
the kingdom of science and jurisprudence.
A more mistaken judgment it would be impossible to form. The only hope for ultimate
peace lies through religion. Knowledge is
not enough. Law is not sufficient. Nothing
suffices but the spirit of God. It is not by
economic readjustments, nor by scientific
discoveries, nor by financial interlocking interests, nor by commercial prudence, nor by
the refinements of art, that the nations are
going to learn war no more, but by a fuller
baptism of the spirit of the man who died on
the cross and who said: "And I, if I be
lifted up, will draw all men unto me." Men
are going to cease trusting in the power of
the mailed fist as they come more and more
under the influence of the naked hand that

was pierced. It is not by might nor by power, that the world is to be conquered, but by my Spirit, saith the Lord.

THE END

BOOKS BY DR. JEFFERSON

QUIET TALKS WITH EARNEST PEOPLE

"A succession of brief conversations in a plain but pithy, bright, and breezy way, which lights up the whole situation with a large and genial good sense. The book deserves wide reading in all denominations."—*The Outlook.*

16mo, cloth. $1.00 *postpaid.*

QUIET HINTS TO GROWING PREACHERS

"It appeals to each reader's good sense and finds corroboration there at every turn. Each chapter bristles with good points."—*Herald and Presbyter.*

16mo, cloth. $1.00 *postpaid.*

THE MINISTER AS PROPHET

"Full of vigor, clearly expressed, and shows a wide knowledge of the needs of men."—*Christian Advocate.*

16mo, cloth. 90 *cents net; by mail,* $1.00.

THE MINISTER AS SHEPHERD

Earnest, eloquent, and sane suggestions as to the scope of the minister's work as pastor or shepherd of his church flock.

16mo, cloth. $1.00 *net; by mail,* $1.10.

DOCTRINE AND DEED

"The profound truths of the Gospel clothed in clear and crisp modern expressions. He is one of the few preachers whose sermons do not lose by being printed and read."—*The Interior.*

12mo, cloth. $1.50 *postpaid.*

THINGS FUNDAMENTAL

"Certainly well worth the study of those who feel that the Bible is losing ground under the scrutiny of science."—*The N. Y. Commercial Advertiser.*

12mo, cloth. $1.50 *net; by mail,* $1.65.

THE CHARACTER OF JESUS

"In point of culture, breadth, and spiritual power, Dr. Jefferson's writings rank among the very highest."—*Boston Herald*.

12mo. cloth. $1.50 *net; by mail,* $1.65.

THE NEW CRUSADE

This book is replete with "straight shots" and striking truths.

12mo, cloth. $1.50 *net; by mail,* $1.65.

MY FATHER'S BUSINESS

Ten sermons for children, in Dr. Jefferson's best style. "A most valuable addition to religious literature for young people."—*Providence News*.

Illustrated. 8vo, cloth. $1.25 *net; by mail,* $1.37.

CHRISTMAS BUILDERS

A beautiful book, tastefully designed and especially suitable for a gift.

With decorations and illustrations. 12mo. 50 cents net; by mail, 56 cents.

THE CAUSE OF THE WAR

"The best exposition of the present situation which has come to my attention," says one who has read it.

Boards, 50 cents net; by mail, 55 cents; paper, 25 cents net; by mail, 28 cents.

THE WORLD'S CHRISTMAS TREE

"A beautiful idea, beautifully set forth."—*The Living Church*.

12mo. 50 cents net; by mail, 56 cents

Published by
THOMAS Y. CROWELL COMPANY